First World War
and Army of Occupation
War Diary
France, Belgium and Germany

58 DIVISION
Divisional Troops
290 Brigade Royal Field Artillery
1 October 1915 - 31 May 1919

WO95/2995/1

The Naval & Military Press Ltd
www.nmarchive.com
Published in association with The National Archives

Published by

The Naval & Military Press Ltd

Unit 10 Ridgewood Industrial Park,
Uckfield, East Sussex,
TN22 5QE England
Tel: +44 (0) 1825 749494

www.naval-military-press.com
www.nmarchive.com

This diary has been reprinted in facsimile from the original. Any imperfections are inevitably reproduced and the quality may fall short of modern type and cartographic standards.

© **Crown Copyright**
Images reproduced by permission of The National Archives, London, England, 2015.

Contents

Document type	Place/Title	Date From	Date To
Miscellaneous	293 Bde R F A Became Army Field Artillery Brigade 1 Army		
Heading	WO95/2995/1		
Heading	58 Division Troops 290 Bde R F A (Formerly 2/1 London Bde) 1915 Oct-1916 Feb		
War Diary	Warren Heath.	01/10/1915	31/10/1915
War Diary	Warren Heath. Ipswich.	06/11/1915	29/11/1915
War Diary	Warren Heath	02/12/1915	11/02/1916
Heading	WO95/2995/2		
Heading	Bef 58 Division Troops 290 Brigade RFA (Formerly 2/1 London BDF) 1917 Jan-1919 Mar		
Heading	War Diary Of 290 Bde RFA 1917 January		
War Diary	Heytesbury	20/01/1917	20/01/1917
War Diary	Havre	22/01/1917	22/01/1917
War Diary	Occoches	28/01/1917	28/01/1917
War Diary	Noeux	05/02/1917	05/02/1917
War Diary	Lucheux	06/02/1917	06/02/1917
War Diary	Heytesbury	20/01/1917	20/01/1917
War Diary	Havre	22/01/1917	22/01/1917
War Diary	Occoches	28/01/1917	28/01/1917
War Diary	Noeux	05/02/1917	05/02/1917
War Diary	Lucheux	06/02/1917	06/02/1917
War Diary	Heytesbury	20/01/1917	20/01/1917
War Diary	Havre	22/01/1917	22/01/1917
War Diary	Occoches	28/02/1917	28/02/1917
War Diary	Noeux	05/02/1917	05/02/1917
War Diary	Lucheux	07/02/1917	24/02/1917
War Diary	La Cauchie	07/03/1917	24/03/1917
War Diary	Boisy St Rictrude	31/03/1917	13/04/1917
War Diary	B.17.b 3.6	14/04/1917	22/04/1917
Heading	War Diary Of 290th Bde. R.S.A. From 3/5/17 To 28/5/17		
War Diary	B.17.B. 3.6.	03/05/1917	17/05/1917
Heading	War Diary Of 290 Bde R.F.A. Vol 6		
War Diary	B.12.d.15.85	20/06/1917	21/06/1917
War Diary	B.17.b.3.6	24/06/1917	26/07/1917
War Diary	Ytres	02/08/1917	05/08/1917
War Diary	Heninel	20/08/1917	21/08/1917
War Diary	Beaurains	26/08/1917	03/09/1917
War Diary	Herzeele	06/09/1917	07/09/1917
War Diary	I.1.9	14/09/1917	14/09/1917
War Diary	Wilsons Farm.	19/09/1917	23/10/1917
War Diary	Cheddar Villa	31/10/1917	13/11/1917
Miscellaneous	D.A.G. 3rd Echelon Base	31/12/1917	31/12/1917
War Diary	Estree Area.	04/12/1917	17/12/1917
War Diary	Cane Post.	12/01/1917	28/02/1917
War Diary	In The Field	01/03/1918	31/03/1918
Heading	Headquarters, 290th Brigade R.F.A. April 1918		
War Diary		01/04/1918	29/07/1918
Heading	290th Brigade. R. F. A. August 1918		

War Diary		31/07/1918	30/11/1918
War Diary	Quevaucamps	01/12/1918	08/03/1919
Heading	WO95/2995/3		
Heading	58 Division Troops 291 Bde RFA (Formerly 2/2 London Bde) 1915 Oct-1916 Feb		
War Diary	Saxmundham	04/10/1915	19/10/1915
War Diary	Woodbridge	20/10/1915	06/02/1916
Heading	WO95/2995/4		
Heading	B E F 58 Division Troops 291 Brigade RFA (Formerly 2/2 London Bde To May 1916) 1917 Jan-1919 May		
Heading	War Diary 291st Bde R.F.A Vol 1 & 2		
War Diary	Heytesbury	22/01/1917	22/01/1917
War Diary	Southampton	22/01/1917	22/01/1917
War Diary	Havre	23/01/1917	24/01/1917
War Diary	Abbeville	25/01/1917	25/01/1917
War Diary	Wavans	26/01/1917	26/01/1917
War Diary	Lucheux	06/02/1917	18/02/1917
War Diary	Bailleulmont	24/02/1917	22/03/1917
Operation(al) Order(s)	Operation Orders No. 5 By Lieut-Colonel W.T. Odam Commanding 291st. Bde. RFA. Appendix A	19/03/1917	19/03/1917
War Diary	Adinfer	22/03/1917	22/03/1917
War Diary	Moyenville	25/03/1917	30/03/1917
War Diary	Battn HQ T25a77 Map 51B S.W.	02/04/1917	02/04/1917
War Diary	Moyenville	03/04/1917	05/04/1917
War Diary	Battn HQ	06/04/1917	13/04/1917
War Diary	Ervillers	14/04/1917	14/04/1917
War Diary	Battn H.Q. at B17b.3.6 Map 57c N.W.	15/04/1917	23/04/1917
Heading	War Diary Of 291st Bde R.F.A. From 3/5/17 To 21/5/17		
War Diary	Battn HQ at B17b 3.6 Map 57c NW	03/05/1917	17/05/1917
War Diary	Battn B17b 3.6	18/05/1917	21/05/1917
Heading	War Diary Of 291 Bde RFA From 29/5/17 To 31/6/17 Vol 6		
War Diary	Battn H.Q. B17b 3.6	20/06/1917	30/06/1917
War Diary	Ervillers	04/07/1917	04/07/1917
War Diary	Fricourt	11/07/1917	11/07/1917
War Diary	Ytres	12/07/1917	18/07/1917
War Diary	Metz En Couture	29/07/1917	29/07/1917
War Diary	Havrincourt	02/08/1917	03/08/1917
War Diary	Boyelle	05/08/1917	07/08/1917
War Diary	St Leger	08/08/1917	26/08/1917
War Diary	Ervillers	26/08/1917	26/08/1917
War Diary	Houpoutre	27/08/1917	27/08/1917
War Diary	Dickebusch	30/08/1917	03/09/1917
War Diary	Nr Herzeele	06/09/1917	07/09/1917
War Diary	Vlamatinge	14/09/1917	14/09/1917
War Diary	La Belle Alliance	20/09/1917	30/09/1917
War Diary	In The Field	04/10/1917	29/10/1917
War Diary	B.H.Q. Vlamertinghe	31/10/1917	02/11/1917
War Diary	Wormhoudt	03/11/1917	03/11/1917
War Diary	Muncq Nieurlet	03/11/1917	03/11/1917
War Diary	B.H.Q. Attin	04/12/1917	04/12/1917
War Diary	Elverdinghe	09/12/1917	09/12/1917
War Diary	Adephe House	10/12/1917	31/12/1917
War Diary	B.H.Q.	12/01/1918	12/01/1918
War Diary	Adelphe House	13/01/1918	13/01/1918

War Diary	Elverdinghe	22/01/1918	23/01/1918
War Diary	Domart	28/01/1918	28/01/1918
War Diary	Carrepuis	29/01/1918	29/01/1918
War Diary	Bretigny	30/01/1918	30/01/1918
War Diary	Vilette	31/01/1918	31/01/1918
War Diary	B.H.Q. Vilette.	01/02/1918	03/02/1918
War Diary	Sinceny	15/02/1918	28/02/1918
War Diary	Elverdinghe	18/01/1918	18/01/1918
War Diary	B.H.Q. Sinceny	01/03/1918	21/03/1918
War Diary	Pierremande	31/03/1918	31/03/1918
Heading	Headquarters 291st Brigade R.F.A. April 1918		
War Diary	BHQ Pierremande	01/04/1918	05/04/1918
War Diary	Boutillerie	06/04/1918	06/04/1918
War Diary	Fouilloy	07/04/1918	30/04/1918
War Diary	B.H.Q. Buigny L'Abbe	03/05/1918	03/05/1918
War Diary	Ponts Remy	16/05/1918	16/05/1918
War Diary	Bourdon	17/05/1918	17/05/1918
War Diary	V15.a.6.3. 57 D	18/05/1918	31/05/1918
War Diary	BHQ Sheet 57 D V.15.a.6.3	01/06/1918	07/06/1918
War Diary	Contay	09/06/1918	09/06/1918
War Diary	St Sauveur	11/06/1918	19/06/1918
War Diary	Bavelincourt	20/06/1918	20/06/1918
War Diary	D.7a.8.7. Sheet 62 D	21/06/1918	30/06/1918
War Diary	D7a.8.7. Sheet 62 N D	01/07/1918	29/07/1918
Heading	291st Brigade. R.F.A. August 1918		
War Diary	B.H.Q. Map Refs Senlis Special Edition Sheets 62D NE 62C NW 1/20,000 Bazieux	01/08/1918	02/08/1918
War Diary	Vaux-Sur-Somme	08/08/1918	08/08/1918
War Diary	Sailly-Laurette	09/08/1918	09/08/1918
War Diary	Malard Wood	10/08/1918	10/08/1918
War Diary	Grenadier Wood Chinelen Valley	11/08/1918	12/08/1918
War Diary	Chinelen Valley	17/08/1918	25/08/1918
War Diary	Maricourt Valley	26/08/1918	27/08/1918
War Diary	Chapelle de Curlu	28/08/1918	30/08/1918
War Diary	Near Hill 110	31/08/1918	31/08/1918
War Diary	BHQ Ref Sheet 62 C Nr Hem	05/09/1918	06/09/1918
War Diary	Aizecourt Le-Bas.	07/09/1918	17/09/1918
War Diary	Quarry E.18c	18/09/1918	24/09/1918
War Diary	Nr Ronssoy	25/09/1918	29/09/1918
War Diary	BHQ. Nr Bellicourt	01/10/1918	01/10/1918
War Diary	Le Catelet	04/10/1918	09/10/1918
War Diary	Aizecourt-Le-Bas	11/10/1918	12/10/1918
War Diary	Maroc	18/10/1918	18/10/1918
War Diary	Dourges.	19/10/1918	19/10/1918
War Diary	Auchy	20/10/1918	20/10/1918
War Diary	Aix	21/10/1918	08/11/1918
War Diary	Wiers	09/11/1918	09/11/1918
War Diary	Ecacheries	11/11/1918	21/11/1918
War Diary	Wiers	29/11/1918	29/11/1918
War Diary	Beloeil	01/12/1918	01/12/1918
War Diary	Belgium	30/12/1918	30/12/1918
War Diary	B.H.Q. Beloeil. Belgium	01/04/1919	30/04/1919
War Diary	B.H.Q. Beloeil Belgium.	01/05/1919	31/05/1919
Heading	WO95/2995/5		
Heading	Trench Mortar Battys. Mar 1917-Dec 1918		
War Diary	Field	01/03/1917	25/03/1917

Heading	War Diary Of 58th DA T. M. B. From 16/5/17 To 31/5/17		
War Diary	Field	16/05/1917	25/06/1917
Heading	War Diary 58th T M. B, From 1st To 31st July 1917 Vol 3		
War Diary	In The Field	03/07/1917	30/07/1917
Heading	58th D.A.T.M. Brigade War Diary For August 1917 Vol 4		
War Diary	In The Sheet 5/c 1/40,000 P33a 3.3	01/08/1917	31/08/1917
Heading	War Diary of 58th D.A.T.M. Bs. September 1917 Vol 5		
War Diary	Sheet 27 D 22c Herzeele	03/09/1917	29/09/1917
Heading	War Diary Of The 58th Divisional Trench Mortar Batteries For October 1917 Vol 6		
War Diary	Sheet 28 A 22d.8.5	02/10/1917	11/10/1917
War Diary	Sheet 28 A 22d 7.2	13/10/1917	28/10/1917
Miscellaneous	War Diary. 58th (London) D.A.C. Month Ending 31/10/17		
Heading	War Diary Of The 58th Divisional Trench Mortar Batteries For The Month Of November 1917 Vol 7		
War Diary	Sheet 28 A 28d 7.2	01/11/1917	30/11/1917
Heading	58th Divisional Trench Mortar Batteries War Diary For December 1917 Vol 8		
War Diary	Longvillers	01/12/1917	12/12/1917
War Diary	Sheet 28 B 15.c.4.7.	12/12/1917	22/12/1917
War Diary	Sheet 28 B 28 Central	23/12/1917	30/12/1917
Heading	War Diary Of The 58th Divisional Trench Mortar Batteries January 1918 Vol 9		
War Diary	Sheet 28 B 28 Central Trois Tours	03/01/1918	20/01/1918
War Diary	Sheet 28 A 22d 7.2	20/01/1918	30/01/1918
Heading	58th Div Trench Mortar Batteries War Diary For February 1918 Vol 10		
War Diary	Chauny	05/02/1918	24/02/1918
Heading	58th Divisional Trench Mortar Batteries War Diary for the Month of March 1918 Vol 11		
War Diary	Chauny	01/03/1918	25/03/1918
War Diary	Blerancourt	26/03/1918	30/03/1918
Heading	58th Divisional Artillery Trench Mortar Batteries. April 1918		
Heading	War Diary Of The 58 Div Arty Trench Mortar Batteries For April 1918 Vol 12		
War Diary	Audignicourt Le Mesnil	01/04/1918	30/04/1918
Heading	58th Divisional Trench Mortar Batteries R.A. War Diary For The Month Of May 1918 Vol 13		
War Diary	Francieres	01/05/1918	15/05/1918
War Diary	U 24d 4.3 Sheet 57 D.	16/05/1918	21/05/1918
War Diary	Warloy	22/05/1918	31/05/1918
Heading	58th Divisional Trench Mortar Batteries R.A. War Diary For The Month Of June 1918 Vol 14		
War Diary	Warloy U 24d 4.3.	01/06/1918	18/06/1918
War Diary	Longpre	18/06/1918	19/06/1918
War Diary	Warloy	20/06/1918	30/06/1918
Heading	58th Div Arty Trench Mortar Batteries War Diary for July 1918 Vol 15		
War Diary	Warloy	01/07/1918	21/07/1918
War Diary	D4c 2.4.	22/07/1918	31/07/1918
Heading	58th Divisional Trench Mortar Officer August 1918		

Heading	58th Divisional Trench Mortar Batteries War Diary For August 1918 Vol 16			
War Diary			01/08/1918	15/08/1918
War Diary	Pont-Noyelles		19/08/1918	27/08/1918
Heading	War Diary Of The 58th Divl T.M. Bs R.A. for the Month Of September 1918 Vol 17			
War Diary	Heilly		03/09/1918	04/09/1918
War Diary	B14d 72		06/09/1918	12/09/1918
War Diary	E7c 22		13/09/1918	28/09/1918
Heading	War Diary Of The 58th Divisional Trench Mortar Batteries R.A. For The Month Of October 1918 Vol 18			
War Diary	Lieramont		03/10/1918	03/10/1918
War Diary	E7c 2.2		06/10/1918	12/10/1918
War Diary	Hersin		13/10/1918	16/10/1918
War Diary	Bully Grenay		17/10/1918	18/10/1918
War Diary	O23.b.4.7.		19/10/1918	19/10/1918
War Diary	Lannay		22/10/1918	22/10/1918
Heading	58th Div. Arty. Trench Mortar Batteries War Diary For The Month Of November 1918 Vol 19			
War Diary	Lannay		03/11/1918	03/11/1918
War Diary	Rongy		04/11/1918	11/11/1918
War Diary	Grandglise G 6c		12/11/1918	20/11/1918
War Diary	Grandglise Sheet 45 G6c		10/12/1918	28/12/1918
Heading	WO95/2995/6			
Heading	58th Divl Ammn Column Jan 1917-1919 May			
War Diary	Winchester		06/01/1917	06/01/1917
War Diary	Southampton		26/01/1917	27/01/1917
War Diary	Harve		28/01/1917	29/01/1917
Heading	War Diary 58th D.A.C. From 1-1-17 To 31-1-17 Vol 1			
War Diary	Southampton		03/02/1917	03/02/1917
War Diary	Harve		04/02/1917	04/02/1917
War Diary	Southampton		04/02/1917	04/02/1917
War Diary	Harve		05/02/1917	05/02/1917
War Diary	Southampton			
War Diary	Mezerolles		06/02/1917	06/02/1917
War Diary	Harve			
War Diary	Mezerolles		07/02/1917	07/02/1917
War Diary	Harve			
War Diary	Mezerolles		08/02/1917	24/02/1917
War Diary	Warlicourt			
War Diary	La Bezeque			
War Diary	Grouches			
War Diary	Warlicourt		25/02/1917	25/02/1917
War Diary	La Bezeque		27/02/1917	28/02/1917
Heading	War Diary 58th D.A.C. From 1-2-17 To 28-2-17 Volume 2			
War Diary	Mezerolles		01/02/1917	28/02/1917
Heading	War Diary. 58th D.A.C. From 1-2-17 To 28-2-17 Vol II			
War Diary	Warlincourt.		01/03/1917	26/03/1917
War Diary	Bienvillers		15/04/1917	15/04/1917
War Diary	Ervilliers		15/04/1917	15/04/1917
Heading	War Diary of 58th D.A.C. From 1/5/17 To 28/5/17 Vol 5			
War Diary	In The Field			
War Diary	In The Field		04/07/1917	07/09/1917
War Diary	Vlamertinghe		02/11/1917	02/11/1917

War Diary	Wormhoudt	03/11/1917	03/11/1917
War Diary	Ruminghem	12/11/1917	12/11/1917
War Diary	Desvres.	13/11/1917	13/11/1917
War Diary	Tubersent	14/11/1917	14/11/1917
War Diary	Frencq	18/11/1917	18/11/1917
War Diary	Maresville	04/12/1917	04/12/1917
War Diary	Merck-St-Lievin	05/12/1917	05/12/1917
War Diary	Lederzeele	06/12/1917	06/12/1917
War Diary	Zermezeele	07/12/1917	29/01/1918
War Diary	Baboeuf	06/02/1918	27/03/1918
Heading	58th Divisional Ammunition Column. April 1918		
War Diary		01/04/1918	11/04/1918
Miscellaneous			
War Diary	Eaucourt Sur Somme	06/05/1918	06/05/1918
War Diary	Bourdon	07/05/1918	07/05/1918
War Diary	Eaucourt Sur Somme	16/05/1918	16/05/1918
War Diary	Belloy	17/05/1918	17/05/1918
War Diary	Contay	24/05/1918	09/06/1918
War Diary	B.9.c	10/06/1918	10/06/1918
War Diary	Longpre	19/06/1918	19/06/1918
War Diary	Picquigny	20/06/1918	30/06/1918
Heading	58th Divisional Ammunition Column. August 1918		
War Diary	Near Contay	03/08/1918	03/08/1918
War Diary	Behencourt	08/08/1918	08/08/1918
War Diary	La Neuville	09/08/1918	09/08/1918
War Diary	Bonnay	12/08/1918	12/08/1918
War Diary	Sailly-le-Sec	27/08/1918	27/08/1918
War Diary	Meaulte	28/08/1918	28/08/1918
War Diary	Etinehem	30/08/1918	30/08/1918
War Diary	Nr Maricourt	05/09/1918	05/09/1918
War Diary	Clery. S. Somme	06/09/1918	06/09/1918
War Diary	Allaines	09/09/1918	30/09/1918
War Diary	Nr Moislains	08/10/1918	08/10/1918
War Diary	Nr Bony	09/10/1918	09/10/1918
War Diary	Nr Driencourt	11/10/1918	12/10/1918
War Diary	Bully Grenay	13/10/1918	13/10/1918
War Diary	Moroc	13/10/1918	13/10/1918
War Diary	Hersin.	18/10/1918	18/10/1918
War Diary	Montigny	19/10/1918	19/10/1918
War Diary	Evin	20/10/1918	20/10/1918
War Diary	La Vacquerie	21/10/1918	21/10/1918
War Diary	Lannay	09/11/1918	09/11/1918
War Diary	Nr Rongy	10/11/1918	10/11/1918
War Diary	Le Croix	11/11/1918	11/11/1918
War Diary	Stambruges	12/11/1918	12/11/1918
War Diary	Grandglise	11/12/1918	11/12/1918
War Diary	Beloeil	01/05/1919	31/05/1919

293 BDE RFA

BECAME ARMY FIELD
ARTILLERY BRIGADE

1 ARMY

Box 2995

NO 95/2995/1

58 DIVISION TROOPS

290 BDE RFA
(FORMERLY 2/1 LONDON BDE)

1915 OCT — 1916 FEB

Box 2995

290 Bde RFA (formerly 2/1 London) WAR DIARY or INTELLIGENCE SUMMARY

Army Form C. 2118

Place	Date	Hour	Summary of Events and Information	Remarks and references to Appendices
Warren Heath.	Oct 1		One Officer and 12 other ranks proceeded to Bordon to take over equipment, etc, of 1/1st London Brigade, R.F.A. (proceeding overseas).	
	" 10		Above party returned.	
	" 26		25 N.C.O's and men sent to Kettering to assist in looking after horses now being used by No.3 Training School. In addition to these, 1 Officer and 15 N.C.O's & men are still at Kettering awaiting leave to bring back horses, guns & equipment of 2/2nd Battery (taken over from 1/2nd Battery, gone overseas.)	
	" 30		61 Horses arrived from Remounts, Kettering.	
	" 31		12 " " " " Wembley.	
			150 " " " " Shirehampton.	

WARREN HEATH CAMP.
31st October 1915.

...................Colonel.
Comdg: 2/1st London Brigade, R.F.A.

Army Form C. 2118.

WAR DIARY

INTELLIGENCE SUMMARY

(Erase heading not required.)

Instructions regarding War Diaries and Intelligence Summaries are contained in F.S. Regs., Part II. and the Staff Manual respectively. Title pages will be prepared in manuscript.

Hour, Date, Place		Summary of Events and Information	Remarks and references to Appendices
Warren Heath, Ipswich.	6/11/15.	45 Horses arrived from Shirehampton.	
"	13/11/15.	33 Horses arrived from Avonmouth.	
"	20/11/15.	The following party returned from Kettering, after attachment to No. 3 Artillery Training School:- Captain S.H.Hurst, 4 N.C.O's, 34 men, 51 horses, 4 Guns & Limbers, 8 wagons & limbers, 1 Box Cart.	
"	29/11/15.	23 Ammunition Wagons. (18pr.) received from Barrow-in-Furness.	

Warren Heath Camp,
Ipswich
30/11/15.

...........Colonel.
Commanding
2/1st London Brigade, R.F.A.

Army Form C. 2118

WAR DIARY
or
INTELLIGENCE SUMMARY
(Erase heading not required.)

Instructions regarding War Diaries and Intelligence Summaries are contained in F. S. Regs., Part II. and the Staff Manual respectively. Title Pages will be prepared in manuscript.

Place	Date	Hour	Summary of Events and Information	Remarks and references to Appendices
Warren Heath	2/12/15		12 18-pr Q.F.Guns & Limbers arrived.	
	3/12/15		13 Wagons & Limbers arrived from Darnall Sheffield.	
	10/12/15		Brigade was inspected by Major General Brunker on Priory Heath.	
	25/12/15		Wire received during afternoon that air raid was expected.	
	28/12/15		Brigade was inspected by Mayor G.O.C. 58th London Division, on Martlesham Heath.	

Warren Heath Camp.

2/1/16

..................Colonel.

Comdg: 2/1st London Brigade, R.F.A.

Secret.

Army Form C. 2118

2/1st London Bde R.F.A.

WAR DIARY
— or —
INTELLIGENCE SUMMARY
(Erase heading not required.)

Instructions regarding War Diaries and Intelligence Summaries are contained in F. S. Regs., Part II. and the Staff Manual respectively. Title Pages will be prepared in manuscript.

Place	Date	Hour	Summary of Events and Information	Remarks and references to Appendices
Warren Heath.	4/1/16		4 15pr Guns & Limbers lent to 2/1st London R.G.A., Hadleigh.	
	7/1/16		2nd Lt L.A.G.Paine proceeded overseas to join 1st Line.	
	13/1/16		19 G.S.Wagons Mark X, arrived from Ordnance.	
	13/1/16		Lieut J.A.Davis proceeded overseas to join 1st Line.	
	14/1/16		4 15pr Guns & 8 Wagons, stores & ammunition, transferred to 2/A Bty H.A.C., Beepham.	
	15/1/16		4 do 8 do to 2/1st Berkshire R.H.A., Puncton.	
	19/1/16		2/3rd Battery left for Orford for Gun Practice on 20/1/16	
	20/1/16		2/1st do 21/1/16	
	21/1/16		2/2nd do 22/1/16	
	23/1/16	12-45 p.m.	Message received from D.H.Q. that a British Byplane would be proceeding between Southend Colchester, Ipswich and Norwich.	
	28/1/16	9-45 p.m.	Message received from Divl. Arty. H.Q. that a Zeppelin was reported, but no need for all ranks to turn out.	
	28/1/16		144,000 rds of .303 S.A.A. transferred to 1/8th Cyclist Battn, Essex Regt, Rayleigh (III Army)	
			144,000 do 2/8th " " " Gt Clacton (III Army)	
	Warren Heath Camp.			
	31.1.16.			

..................Colonel.

Comdg: 2/1st London Brigade, R.F.A.

SECRET.

Army Form C. 2118.

WAR DIARY
of
INTELLIGENCE SUMMARY

(Erase heading not required.)

Instructions regarding War Diaries and Intelligence Summaries are contained in F. S. Regs., Part II. and the Staff Manual respectively. Title pages will be prepared in manuscript.

Hour, Date, Place	Summary of Events and Information	Remarks and references to Appendices
February.		
Warren Heath. 10th 3 p.m.	British byplane passed over camp from N.W. to S.E. flying low.	
11th	4 15 pr Guns & Limbers returned from 2/1st London R.G.A., Hadleigh.	

Warren Heath Camp.
29. 2. 16.

..................Colonel.
Comdg: 2/1st London Brigade, R.F.A.

WO 95/2995/2

BEF

58 DIVISION TROOPS

290 BRIGADE RFA
(FORMERLY 2/1 LONDON BDE)

1917 JAN — 1919 MAR

Box 2995

Vol #2
#3

WAR DIARY
OF
290 BDE RFA.
1917 JANUARY

Army Form C. 2118.

WAR DIARY
or
INTELLIGENCE SUMMARY.
(Erase heading not required.)

29th R.F.A

Instructions regarding War Diaries and Intelligence Summaries are contained in F. S. Regs., Part II. and the Staff Manual respectively. Title pages will be prepared in manuscript.

Place	Date	Hour	Summary of Events and Information	Remarks and references to Appendices
Southampton	20/1/17	10 p.m	Brigade left Southampton for France.	
Havre	22/1/17	10 p.m.	Left Havre 23/1/17 for Auxi-le-Château & billeted at BEAUCHES.	
Beauches	23/1/17	1 pm	Occupied billets at NOEUX.	
Havre	5/2/17	11 am	Occupied billets at LUCHEUX.	
Lucheux	8/2/17		"D" Battery converted into a 6 gun Battery.	
	24/2/17			

H Sheppard Lt Col
Cmdg 29th Bde R.F.A.

Army Form C. 2118.

WAR DIARY
or
INTELLIGENCE SUMMARY.
(Erase heading not required.)

Instructions regarding War Diaries and Intelligence Summaries are contained in F. S. Regs., Part II. and the Staff Manual respectively. Title pages will be prepared in manuscript.

Place	Date	Hour	Summary of Events and Information	Remarks and references to Appendices
Shoreham	30/1/17	10 pm	Ringold left Southampton for France	
Havre	30/1/17	10 am	Left Havre 30/1/17 for Rouen	
Coisels	20/1/17	1 pm	Grateful Killed at MOEUX	
Moeux	5/2/17	11 am	Grateful Killed at LUCHEUX	
Lucheux	8/2/17	—	"B" Battery converted into a 6 gun Battery	

34b/1/7

290th Bde R.F.A.

WAR DIARY
or
INTELLIGENCE SUMMARY.
(Erase heading not required.)

Army Form C. 2118.

Place	Date	Hour	Summary of Events and Information	Remarks and references to Appendices
Blaydesley	20/2/17	10 pm	Brigade left Southampton for France	
Havre	22/2/17	10 pm	Left Havre 22/2/17 for Oeust-le-Chateau, 1 killed at Occoches.	
Occoches	2/3/17	11 am	Brigade billeted at NOEUX.	
Noeux	5/3/17	11 am	Brigade billeted at LUCHEUX.	
Lucheux	11/3/17	12 noon	"D" Battery converted into a 6 gun Howr Battery.	

20/3/17

Lt Colonel for A.E.J.
Cdg 290th Bde R.F.A.

WAR DIARY
or
INTELLIGENCE SUMMARY.

Army Form C. 2118.

Place	Date	Hour	Summary of Events and Information	Remarks and references to Appendices
Lucheux	24/2/17	3pm	Brigade returned the 245th Bde R.F.A. in the first instance and Headquarters at LA-CAUCHIE	Bttys by stry dypt
La Cauchie	25/2/17	4pm	Received information that MONCHY had been vacated by the Enemy.	Bttys by stry dypt
La Cauchie	25/2/17		B/290th Bty advanced & took up position at S.11.D. 15 38	51 B.S.W Bttys by stry dypt
La Cauchie	26/2/17		Lt. Col. H.P. Clarke assumed command of B/290th Bty and C/291st Bty. Established Headquarters at S.14.C.4.5	51.B.S.W Bttys by stry dypt
La Cauchie	26/2/17		O.C. R.F.A. Baldwin 306th Bde R.F.A. not in action from 19-3-17	Bttys by stry dypt
	27/2/17			

for Brig any comdg 306 Bde R.F.A.
Cdg 306th Bde R.F.A.

WAR DIARY
or
INTELLIGENCE SUMMARY.
(Erase heading not required.)

Army Form C. 2118.

290 Bde R.F.A.
5/Lond
Vol 4

Place	Date	Hour	Summary of Events and Information	Remarks and references to Appendices
La Cauchie	29/3/17		HQrs established at BOIRY-ST-RICTRUDE.	HQ & R/290
Boiry St Rictrude	3/3/17		C & D Batteries went into action.	HQ & C/290 HQ & D/290
	7/4/17		Group under command of Col H.R. Clark, composed of A, B, C, D/290th + C/291st Bty, Leonards which Infantry attacked HENIN-ST-COTEUL + CROISILLES	HQ & A/290 HQ & B/290
	12/4/17		A, B, C & D Batteries came out of action.	HQ & A/290 HQ & B/290
	13/4/17		Brigade proceeded to Bivouacs at B.26.H.O.9 + HQrs established at B.1. d. 3.6.	C 7.c.3.3 HQ & A/290 B 1.c.9. C 7.c.9. B/290. C 7.c.3.1 C/290. B.12. d. 3.2 D/290.
Bty S & 3	14/4/17		A, B, C & D Batteries in action at	HQ & A/290
	19/4/17		A & D Batteries out of action & proceeded to Wagon lines at B.26 H O 9	HQ & A/290 HQ & D/290
	22/4/17		B & C Batteries out of action & proceeded to Wagon lines at B.26. H. O. 9	HQ & B/290 HQ & C/290
	22/4/17		A & D Batteries in action at above position	HQ & A/290 HQ & D/290 C/290 B/290 R.F.A

Vol 5

CONFIDENTIAL
****

WAR DIARY

OF

290th Bde. R.F.A.

From 3/5/17
To 28/5/17

Army Form C. 2118.

WAR DIARY
or
INTELLIGENCE SUMMARY.
(Erase heading not required.)

Place	Date	Hour	Summary of Events and Information	Remarks and references to Appendices
B.17.b.3.6.	2/5/17	3-30 a.m	58th Div'l Arty Group Barrage whilst Infantry delivered attack on BULLECOURT	1st Attempt by 7th Bde.
	10/5/17		58th Division in action night 15/16th May, 1917.	1st Attempt by 7th Bde.
	17/5/17		58th Div'l Arty Barrage whilst Infantry attack & capture BULLECOURT VILLAGE	1st Attempt by 1st Bde.

[signed] Capt & Adjt, 290 Bde 58 Div. R.F.A.
Copy of 290 Bde 58 Div. R.F.A.

28/5/17

1916

Confidential

War Diary
of
290 Bde. RFA

Army Form C. 2118.

WAR DIARY
or
INTELLIGENCE SUMMARY.
(Erase heading not required.)

Instructions regarding War Diaries and Intelligence Summaries are contained in F. S. Regs., Part II. and the Staff Manual respectively. Title pages will be prepared in manuscript.

Place	Date	Hour	Summary of Events and Information	Remarks and references to Appendices
B.2.d.15.88.			Section of D/290 Bty advanced to C.22.d.26.40	
B.7.6.8.6.	24/6/17 10 a.m.		290th Bde & 291st Bde R.F.A. formed Right Group Artillery, command taken over from Oldags 55th Divl Arty by Oldage 7th Divl Arty. 10 Bdeg of Art Pty	

Original

290 Brigade RFA.

Army Form C. 2118.

290 Bde Lit 2 of

Lot 7

WAR DIARY
or
INTELLIGENCE SUMMARY.
(Erase heading not required.)

Instructions regarding War Diaries and Intelligence Summaries are contained in F. S. Regs., Part II. and the Staff Manual respectively. Title pages will be prepared in manuscript.

Place	Date	Hour	Summary of Events and Information	Remarks and references to Appendices
E.D.F.36	[date]		Commencement of the relief of the Brigade by 172nd Bde RFA	
			Completion of the relief by the 172 Bde Staff	1st Bty by one by D/172
			Brigade moved to Aveluy Wood at B.25.c.1.8	A/ Bty relieved by A/172
				B/ Bty relieved by B/172
			Brigade moved to Argonnes at P.33.c.m	C/ Bty relieved by C/172
			Brigade billeted at Argonnes	D/ Bty relieved by D/172
5.P.M.			One section of each battery billeted between the 157th Brigade	E/ Bty relieved by E/172
			Commencement of the two nice move from Argonnes	F/ Bty relieved by F/172
				B/ Bty relieved by B/172
			Headquarters of Brigade moved to D.27.c.3.4	C/ Bty relieved by C/172
11pm			One half of the two sections of each battery arrived	D/ Bty relieved by D/172

WAR DIARY
INTELLIGENCE SUMMARY.
(Erase heading not required.)

Army Form C. 2118.

Instructions regarding War Diaries and Intelligence Summaries are contained in F. S. Regs., Part II. and the Staff Manual respectively. Title pages will be prepared in manuscript.

Place	Date	Hour	Summary of Events and Information	Remarks and references to Appendices
	July 4th		Relief of the Brigade by the 29 to Brigade completed. 1st Bhagalpur Battery	
	do		Brigade Head quarters moved to Magaphia 1 Bty Magh Battery	
	25.7.04		Bde. H.Q. Btys moved into billets under the orders of 10th Magh Bde. Mag.	
			28/5/17	

6 Mag 69 Bde RFA
CRA 1 Mag

Com 19 eyes a Brigade RFA

WAR DIARY
or
INTELLIGENCE SUMMARY.
(Erase heading not required.)

Army Form C. 2118.

290 Bde R.F.A. Vol 8

Place	Date	Hour	Summary of Events and Information	Remarks and references to Appendices
YTRES	2/8/17 5/8/17		Brigade moved to new position at HENINEL and relieved the 50th Bde R.F.A. in action on 5/8/17. Brigade H.Qrs at N.32.c.7.7. Wagon line in M.17. a + c.	
			W.A. Hazenby Capt & Adjt	
HENINEL	night of 20/8/17 21/8/17		Brigade relieved by 22nd A.F.A. Bde and proceeded to Wagon line in M.17. a + c.	
			W.A. Hazenby Capt & Adjt	
BEAURAINS	night of 28/8/17 29/8/17		Brigade entrained at ARRAS and detrained 29/8/17 at GODEWAERSVELDE.	
			W.A. Hazenby Capt & Adjt	
	30/8/17		Wagon line taken up at G.32.a. Central.	
			W.A. Hazenby Capt & Adjt	
	30/8/17	2 pm	Brigade moved to Wagon line at H.25.d.5.3. relieved by 82 Bde R.F.A.	
			W.A. Hazenby Capt & Adjt	
	31/8/17		"A" "B" "C" Batteries commenced to relieve the 1st Australian Field Arty in action. Battery positions in I.24.A. and I.17.C.	
			W.A. Hazenby Capt & Adjt	

290th Brigade R.F.A.

WAR DIARY
or
INTELLIGENCE SUMMARY.
(Erase heading not required.)

Army Form C. 2118.

Vol 9

Place	Date	Hour	Summary of Events and Information	Remarks and references to Appendices
	3-9-17		Brigade relieved by 110th Brigade R.F.A. and proceeded to Wagon Lines at HERZEELE. B. Haggerty Capt. & Adjt.	
HERZEELE	6-9-17		Brigade left Wagon Lines at HERZEELE and relieved 102 Brigade R.F.A. 1 Section per Battery in action 6/7th.	
	7-9-17		Rest of Brigade followed 7-9-17 and relief of 102 Brigade completed by noon 7-9-17. Wagon Lines at H.1.b. and B.25.d. Headquarters at I.1.d. B. Haggerty Capt. & Adjt.	
I.1.a.	14-9-17		Headquarters moved to WILSONS FARM. Command of Right Group, 58th Divisional Artillery - consisting of 290th Brigade R.F.A. and 155 A.F.A Brigade - taken over relieving 153rd A.F.A. Brigade. B. Haggerty Capt. & Adjt.	

Army Form C. 2118.

290th Brigade R.F.A

WAR DIARY
or
INTELLIGENCE SUMMARY.
(Erase heading not required.)

Instructions regarding War Diaries and Intelligence Summaries are contained in F. S. Regs., Part II. and the Staff Manual respectively. Title pages will be prepared in manuscript.

Place	Date	Hour	Summary of Events and Information	Remarks and references to Appendices
WILSONS FARM	19/20		Barrage and attack by 58th Division. 6th Major & Capt & Adjt	
	25/26		Barrage and attack by 58th Division. 6th Major & Capt & Adjt	
"	27/28		84th A.F.A. Brigade relieved 153rd A.F.A Brigade in its right Group. 6th Major & Capt & Adjt	
"	30/9/		Right Group Command taken over by 84th A.F.A Brigade. 290th Brigade Headquarters moved to I.1.d. 6th Major Capt & Adjt	

290th Brigade R.F.A.

WAR DIARY

Army Form C. 2118.

Sept 1st to Oct 10

Place	Date	Hour	Summary of Events and Information	Remarks and references to Appendices
	17/10/17		Brigade Headquarters moved to CHEDDAR VILLA. C.17.C.75.00.	Oct 17
			E.J.Thynne Capt & Adjt	
	18/10/17		Command of No. 3 Group (290th and 291st Brigades R.F.A.), 9th Divisional Artillery taken over.	
			E.J.Thynne Capt & Adjt	
	23/10/17		Wagon Lines moved from B.2.s.d. to C.2.s.c. CANAL BANK.	
			E.J.Thynne Capt & Adjt	
			Operations in the YPRES Battle were carried out on 4th, 12th, 21st, 25th, and 30th October.	
			E.J.Thynne Capt & Adjt	

Army Form C. 2118.

290th Brigade R.F.A.
WAR DIARY
or
INTELLIGENCE SUMMARY
(Erase heading not required.)

Place	Date	Hour	Summary of Events and Information	Remarks and references to Appendices
CHEDDAR VILLA	1917 2/10/17		Brigade Headquarters moved to Wagon Lines at Canal Bank on being relieved by 1st Div. Arty. William Heye Major Capt. RAH- at Poliniques	
	290nd Bar		Brigade proceeded to Bulloh spending the night at WORMHOUDT.	
	12/13th Nov.		Brigade proceeded to Bulloh en route to ESQUIRE AREA spending the night at DESVRES. Brigade Headquarters established at MONT CAVREL. William Heye Capt. Adjt. 290nd Brigade RFA	

William Heye Capt. Adjt.
290nd Brigade RFA

D.A.G.
3rd Echelon. Base

4

Herewith War Diary of this Brigade for December 1917.

In the Field
31-12-17

[signature] Capt. & Adjt
for Lt. Col.
Comdg 290 Bde R.F.A

Army Form C. 2118.

WAR DIARY
or
INTELLIGENCE SUMMARY.
(Erase heading not required.)

Instructions regarding War Diaries and Intelligence Summaries are contained in F. S. Regs., Part II. and the Staff Manual respectively. Title pages will be prepared in manuscript.

Place	Date	Hour	Summary of Events and Information	Remarks and references to Appendices
ESTREE AREA	4/2/17		Brigade proceeded from ESTREE Area by road and occupied billets at MERCK ST LIEVIN for the night.	By Majority Capt. & Adjt.
	5/2/17		Brigade continued its march to forward area billeting for the night at BROXEELE.	By Majority Capt. & Adjt.
	6/2/17		March continued and billets occupied for the night at ZERNEZEELE.	By Majority Capt. & Adjt.
	7/2/17		Brigade continued march and occupied wagon lines at ELVERDINGHE.	By Majority Capt. & Adjt.
	8/2/17		One Section of each Battery of the Brigade relieved the 62nd and 63rd Brigades in action.	By Majority Capt. & Adjt.

290 Brigade R.F.A.

WAR DIARY
or
INTELLIGENCE SUMMARY.

Army Form C. 2118.

(Erase heading not required.)

Place	Date	Hour	Summary of Events and Information	Remarks and references to Appendices
	9/9/17		Relief of 82nd and 83rd Brigades completed. Batte. Headquarters established at CANE POST (C.9.a.5.5.) Ref. Map. St JULIEN 28 N.W.2 (noted).	
	11/9/17		Brigade Wagon Lines moved to C.26.c. (Ref. St JULIEN 28 NW2.) 1/10,000	

F.H. Maynard. Capt. & Adjt.
290 Brigade R.F.A.

F.H. Maynard. Capt. & Adjt.
290 Brigade R.F.A.

290th Brigade RFA

WAR DIARY
or
INTELLIGENCE SUMMARY.
(Erase heading not required.)

Army Form C. 2118.

Place	Date	Hour	Summary of Events and Information	Remarks and references to Appendices
CANE POST.	June 12/13th		Brigade relieved in action by 157th Brigade R.F.A.	Lt. Colonel D.S.O.
	14th		One Section per Battery on night of 12/13th relieved, the remaining sections on night of 13/14th. Command passing to the 157th Brigade on the morning of 14.6.14 — when the Brigade moves to Wagon Lines in HAMHOEK AREA.	
	15th		Lt. Colonel A.H. Clark D.S.O. relinquished command of Brigade	Lt. Colonel D.S.O. Lt. Colonel D.S.O.
	16th		Lt. Colonel W.A.F. James D.S.O. assumed Command of Brigade	Lt. Colonel D.S.O.
	22nd		Brigade entrained at PROVEN to proceed to 3rd Army Area	Lt. Colonel D.S.O.
	25th		Brigade detained at VILLERS BRETONNEUX and proceeds to Billets in HANGARD.	Lt. Colonel D.S.O.

290th Brigade RFA

WAR DIARY
or
INTELLIGENCE SUMMARY.
(Erase heading not required.)

Army Form C. 2118.

Place	Date	Hour	Summary of Events and Information	Remarks and references to Appendices
	Jany 28th		Brigade marched from HANGARD to the forward area spending the night at GRUNY.	Lt Colonel DSO
	" 29th		Brigade continued the march to forward area and occupied billets in BABŒUF.	Lt Colonel DSO
	" 30th		Brigade Headquarters transferred to LIEZ. "A" "B" and "C" Batteries relieved the 221st Regiment of French Artillery in the line.	Lt Colonel DSO
	31st		Lt. Colonel W.A.F. Jones DSO. took over Command of Group of Artillery consisting of A/290, B/290, C/290, and D and Z Batteries of the 3rd Army Brigade RHA.	Lt Colonel DSO 290 Brigade RFA

W.A.F. Jones
Lt Colonel
Comdg 290 Brigade RFA

Army Form C. 2118.

290 Bde R.F.A.

J 14

WAR DIARY or INTELLIGENCE SUMMARY.
(Erase heading not required.)

Instructions regarding War Diaries and Intelligence Summaries are contained in F.S. Regs., Part II. and the Staff Manual respectively. Title pages will be prepared in manuscript.

Place	Date	Hour	Summary of Events and Information	Remarks and references to Appendices
	Feb. 16		General Bell, United States Army, inspected some of the Battery positions.	
	Feb. 17		Working party consisting of 3 officers and 110 men of the 83rd Brigade R.F.A. (18th Div.) reported for work on new position.	
	Feb. 21		Captain R.M. Harman, R.F.A, was posted to Command B/290, vice Captain (T/Major) J.E. Meadows temporarily transferred to D.A.C. pending further posting.	
	Feb. 22		Major J.L. Caprive M.C. R.F.A reported for a month's attachment to B.H.Q.	
	Feb. 24		5th Bay Brigade R.F.A. (Quessy Sector) and 290th Brigade R.F.A. (VENDEUIL Sector) completed first half of mutual relief.	
	Feb. 25		Second half of relief completed, 290th Brigade taking over defence of QUESSY sector from 6 pm, Brigade Headquarters at QUESSY covering the 195th Infantry Brigade.	
	Feb. 26		Captain J.C. Mant, R.F.A posted to Command of C/290, vice Lieut (T/Major) W.H. Swan.	
	Feb. 27		Lieut (T/Major) W.H. Swan wounded and evacuated.	
	Feb. 28		In consequence of German activity on the French front, C/290 ordered to position south of the river to support 291st B.G. This order was cancelled later, but began relief of Brigade staff by harnessed up until midnight. Quiet night.	

C.O. 290th Brigade R.F.A.

28.2.18.

Army Form C. 2118.

58/3m

WAR DIARY
MARCH, 1918

INTELLIGENCE SUMMARY. 290 Bde. R.F.A.

(Erase heading not required.)

Instructions regarding War Diaries and Intelligence Summaries are contained in F. S. Regs., Part II. and the Staff Manual respectively. Title pages will be prepared in manuscript.

Place	Date	Hour	Summary of Events and Information	Remarks and references to Appendices
In the Field.	MARCH 1918. 1 to 20.		All batteries of 1/B Brigade engaged in constructing and improving position in defence of Battle Zone. Harassing fire nightly on ST. FIRMIN & LA FÈRE. Lt.Col. JONES D.S.O. WAR evacuated to England on 13th. Major F.L. CONGREVE assumed command of the Brigade. Lt. G. RUSSELL proceeded on 14 days leave to England on 17th, 2t. HARTFIELD became A/Adjt.	
	21	3.45/- 4.5 AM 4.10 AM 7.10 AM	"Counter Preparation" carried out by all Batteries. Enemy bombardment began. Brigade again fired on "Counter Preparation" Enemy reported in Picketfields on West side of OISE & SOMBRE canal 1/2 mile ST. FIRMIN South. Concentration of all batteries ordered on West bank of canal. Communication with batteries now only by orderlies.	
		9.30 AM	A/290 Forward Gun destroyed & detachment withdrawn after firing about 200 rounds. Situation obscure owing to dense mist. Nothing heard of B/290's Forward Section all day.	
		11.15 AM 11.15 - 7.30 PM	Enemy massing behind FERME ROUGE (E. of road QUESSY - FARGUIEZ) - batteries ordered to fire on them. Every then time refused by artillery attempts to debouch from FERME ROUGE	

Army Form C. 2118.

WAR DIARY MARCH, 1918 (cont.)
INTELLIGENCE SUMMARY 290 Brigade R.F.A.
(Erase heading not required.)

Place	Date	Hour	Summary of Events and Information	Remarks and references to Appendices
MARCH (cont)	21	1 p.m.	D/R.H.A. reported to Bde. But ink action at VOUEL-TERGNIER Cross roads. Enemy in DISTILLERY at FARGNIERS.	
		4 p.m.		
		8.15 p.m.	After broke enemy succeeded in capturing B/290's 4-gun position & FORT LIEZ B/290 Guns destroyed by 106 HE, In consequence of capture of FORT LIEZ A/290 & D/290 ordered to withdraw 4 guns C/290 destroyed & detachments withdrawn. A/290 & D/290 ordered to withdraw. 290 Bde H.Q. moved to VIRY –	
		11.30 p.m.	Enemy holding line of CROZAT canal at QUESSY.	
			NO REVIER.	
		11 pm.	Batteries in action in BOIS MALLOT – A/290 5 guns, C/290 2 guns (withdrawn from CONDREN) D/RHA 6 guns, D/290 4 hours. It was impossible to withdraw forward section of D/290 owing to roads being destroyed they by shell fire. The 2 hows here therefore blown up.	
			CASUALTIES. "T" Capt. Hicks & 2 LT. H. FANG (B/290) missing believed captured, 1 S.O.R. missing; killed 4 O.R.; wounded 2 LT. F.D. KEANE + 100 O.R. – Horses 12 killed; 4 wounded	
	22	6.30 p.m.	Batteries of Brigade in TERGNIER & fired in tensile retired by R.H.Q. on F.O.O's H/Qtrs check batteries moved to ROUEZ area – B.H.Q. moved to CHAUNY.	
	23	3 AM.	Rolling barrage commenced with object of driving enemy back over CROZAT canal.	

Army Form C. 2118.

WAR DIARY MARCH, 1918

INTELLIGENCE SUMMARY. 290 Brigade R.F.A.

(Erase heading not required.)

Place	Date	Hour	Summary of Events and Information	Remarks and references to Appendices
March (cont.)	23rd (cont.)	10:30	French Infantry retired in FRIÈRES WOOD.	
		11:30 AM	12 inch How. in Neihron mounting attacked to 9 grp – given BUTTE as target – retired 4:30 p.m.	
		12:30 p.m	O/R.H.A. detached from group.	
		1:10 pm.	Batteries (A/290 5 guns, C/290 2 guns, D/290 4 hows) ordered to retire on VILLEQUIER-AUMONT – Rue de CAUMONT. Positions taken up by A/C/D/290 between CAUMONT + RUE de CAUMONT. Objective East of road VIRY-NEUREUIL-NOUREUIL.	
	24th	2 A.M.	Bde. H.Q. moved to ABBÉCOURT	
		9 A.M.	B/290 moved to QUIERZY	
		6 A.M.	2 – 18 prs. C/290 out of action (buffer trouble). Group now = A/290 5 guns, D/290 4 – 4"5 hows. Enemy reported in BETHANCOURT-en-VAUX. A/290 + D/290 withdrew to positions between CRÉPIGNY + MONDESCOURT. CAUMONT evacuated. Further withdrawal to positions between BÉTHANCOURT + NEUFLIEUX. Further advance of enemy caused withdrawal of both batteries to BABŒUF.	
	25th	Noon	H.Q. moved to RUE MILLON. Acting in orders from C.R.A. 18th D.A. Batteries moved South of River OISE during night of 24/25 March. A/290 + D/290 took up positions 1000x S.E. of VARESNES. These	

WAR DIARY
INTELLIGENCE SUMMARY. 290 Brigade R.F.A.

MARCH, 1918

Army Form C. 2118.

Place	Date	Hour	Summary of Events and Information	Remarks and references to Appendices
March (cont)	25 (cont)		positions becoming untenable. A/290 moved during night to RUE MILLON and	
	26th	10 AM	in Kaving (26th) 8 Cwts. Thence A-D/290 moved to positions in Bois de MANICAMP where they remained until 58th D.A. was moved from area on April 2nd	
		Mid'nt	H.Q. moved from RUE MILLON to BESMÉ. 2 sections each of 407, 408 R.F.A., 3.18pr. A/291, 2.18pr. B/291, 1-18pr. C/291 & 4.4.5How D/291 came into action in area Bois de FÊVE under orders of O.C. 290 Bde.	
	27th	Night	Most of these guns were engaged to East side of OISE & AISNE canal leaving 1-18pr. A/291 & 2-How D/291 under command of O.C. 290 Bde. These guns remained until props came out of action on April 2. Harassing fire was carried out by day and (chiefly) by night on enemy's communications CHAUNY-MAREST-DAM PCOUV2 T.	
	28		B/290 - reconstituted as 4 gun battery came into action at BAC d'ARBLINCOURT under orders of O.C. 291 Bde. R.F.A. The guns (one section each of 407, 408 R.F.A.) were taken over in action.	
	29 30 31		Usual harassing fire on enemy's lines of communication in Brigade Zone.	

W.M. Jones Lt Col
O.C. 290th Bde R.F.A.

58th Div.

WAR DIARY

Headquarters,

290th BRIGADE, R.F.A.

A P R I L

1 9 1 8

Army Form C. 2118.

WAR DIARY
2nd Brigade R.H.A.
INTELLIGENCE SUMMARY.
(Erase heading not required)

July 16

Place	Date	Hour	Summary of Events and Information	Remarks and references to Appendices
	1/4/18		Headquarters BESCHÉ, Battery in action FÈVE WOOD, "C" Battery brought two guns into action having been out of action for a week.	
	2/4/18		Headquarters and Batteries moved to BERLANCOURT in the evening, the French Batteries covering the front we vacated.	
	3/4/18		The Brigade marched to VILLERS-COTTERETS and LONG POINT, "A" and "C" Batteries to the former place H.Q., "B" and "D" Batteries to the latter, starting at 8 p.m.	
	4/4/18		Entrained for AMIENS.	
	5/4/18		Brigade detrained at LONGEAU between 2 a.m. and 12 noon and camped on the BOULEVARDS, AMIENS.	
	6/4/18		OC Brigade and Battery Commanders proceeded to inspect battery positions near FOUILLOY, "A" Battery and 1 section each of B.C. and D. Batteries went into action after dark, relieving Batteries of the 177th Brigade, the Brigade now coming under orders of 5 Australian Division R.A.	
	7/4/18		Relief completed, remaining section of "B" "C" and "D" going into action after dark.	

Army Form C. 2118.

Page II.

WAR DIARY
290 Brigade R.F.A
INTELLIGENCE SUMMARY.

(Erase heading not required.)

Instructions regarding War Diaries and Intelligence Summaries are contained in F.S. Regs., Part II. and the Staff Manual respectively. Title pages will be prepared in manuscript.

Place	Date	Hour	Summary of Events and Information	Remarks and references to Appendices
	9/4/18		Battery positions heavily shelled from 4 am to 7 am, front system also shelled with gas shell. 2/Lieut L. Hart gassed at Brigade O.P. and admitted to Hospital. A large number of officers who had been detained at the Base since the beginning of the Push rejoined the Brigade.	
	10/4/18		One gun of A Battery brought into action in a forward position as an anti-tank gun.	
	11-17/4/18		Very little hostile action (?).	
	18/4/18		Commenced mutual relief with the 298th Army Brigade in the VILLERS-BRETONNEUX Sector.	
	19/4/18		Relief completed guns handed over in situ, the Brigade coming under orders of 56th D.A. covering front held by the 8th Divn. Infantry. 169th and 290th Brigades, having Headquarters at I.73 Infantry Brigade Headquarters.	
	23/4/18		Lt. Colonel JONES D.S.O. took command of the Group composed of 96th	

page 3

WAR DIARY
290th Brigade R.F.A.
INTELLIGENCE SUMMARY

Place	Date	Hour	Summary of Events and Information	Remarks and references to Appendices
	24/4/18		German attack on our sector commencing with a very heavy bombardment at 4 a.m., between 12 noon and 2 p.m. Batteries were withdrawn to rear positions, leaving 5 shots and 1-18 pdr. At 10 p.m. a counter attack was made, the enemy being driven back to his starting point, and at some points further, the 5 shots and 1-18pdr being recovered. During the day Majors Newman and Moore and 2nd Lts Mactier, Miles and Parson were wounded and admitted to hospital. 2/Lt Wright who went forward during the morning was wounded and captured. Casualties: 6 Officers and 64 O.R's.	
	25/4/18		Mutual relief carried out with 82nd Brigade in the afternoon, the 290 Brigade going to reserve positions in T.3.	
	28/4/18		Colonel W.H.F. Jones D.S.O. reported and took command of the Brigade on Jones' Group ceasing to exist. At 8.30 p.m. Headquarters and all Batteries were withdrawn to Wagon Lines near CAGNY.	
	29-30/4/18		Brigade proceeded by route march to rest area in EPAGNE and EPAGNETTE, leaving the night of —	

Army Form C. 2118.

WAR DIARY
or
INTELLIGENCE SUMMARY.
(Erase heading not required.)

Place	Date	Hour	Summary of Events and Information	Remarks and references to Appendices
CROUY	29.30.4.16		Brigade Headquarters established at CHATEAU EPAGNE during the afternoon of 16. 30th Total casualties for the month 7 officers and 75 other ranks.	

N.G. Jones.
Lt-Colonel RSD
Commanding
90 Brigade RFA

Army Form C. 2118.

290 Brigade R.F.A.

WAR DIARY
or
INTELLIGENCE SUMMARY.
(Erase heading not required)

Place	Date	Hour	Summary of Events and Information	Remarks and references to Appendices
	May 1-16		Brigade remained at Rest in ERAGNE and EPAGNETTE.	
	3rd		2/Lt Allsopp to Taylor M.C. posted to Brigade to Gunmount B/290.	
	11th		"B" Battery proceeded by road to SAILLY-le-SEC to act as depot Battery at the Reserve Army Artillery School.	
	13th		Major General C.E.D. Budworth C.B., C.M.G., M.V.O. R.A., G.O.C. R.A. Fourth Army, inspected Gun Parks, Horse lines and horses in the morning and attended the 58th Divisional Artillery Horse Show in the afternoon.	
	16th		Brigade less B/290, proceeded by route march and spent the night at BOURDON.	
	17		Brigade continued the route march and occupied the Wagon Lines of the 169th Brigade R.F.A. in the neighbourhood of RAVELINCOURT, one section of each battery relieving the 169th Brigade R.F.A. in the line.	

II 290 Brigade R.F.A.

WAR DIARY
or
INTELLIGENCE SUMMARY.

Army Form C. 2118.

Place	Date	Hour	Summary of Events and Information	Remarks and references to Appendices
	May 1918			290 Brigade R.F.A.
	21		Reviewing two sections of each Battery relieved its 169th Brigade R.F.A. Brigade Headquarters moved to HENENCOURT CHATEAU. Lt Colonel N.A.F. JONES. D.S.O. taking over its defence of the line, covering, with the following Batteries, A/290, C/290, D/290 and 407th Battery, 1500 yards of the front due N. of ALBERT.	
	22		Major General VAUGHAN, Inspector General of Horse Management inspected all horses of the Brigade in its Wagon Lines.	
	23		The following Awards were made:- Mentioned in Despatches. 2/Lieut. L.F. Robinson. Military Medal. 925611. Gunner. Clarkson. R. 95062. Gunner. Humphrey. P. 926161. Driver. Ruddle. H. 925793. Driver. Castle. W.P. 690402. L/Bdr. Hodgkinson. P. 94409. Gunner. Martin. A. 925619. Gunner. Templeman. E.W.	

Sheet III

290 Brigade R.F.A.

WAR DIARY
or
INTELLIGENCE SUMMARY.

Army Form C. 2118.

Place	Date	Hour	Summary of Events and Information	Remarks and references to Appendices
	May 23		Awards (contd) Bar to Military Medal. 30796. A/4/Bdr. T. Hutchings M.M.	
	24/25		407th Battery relieved by A/236.	
	28/29		A/236 Battery relieved by A/83.	

W. R. Jones
Lt Colonel D.S.O.
Commanding
290 Brigade R.F.A.

WAR DIARY

290 Brigade R.F.A.

INTELLIGENCE SUMMARY.

Vol 18

Army Form C. 2118.

Place	Date	Hour	Summary of Events and Information	Remarks and references to Appendices
1918	June 1st		2/Lieut. L.F.BECKH. joined the Brigade and was posted to A/290. Headquarters 18th Divisional Artillery relieved Headquarters of the 58th Divisional Artillery in the Line.	
	2nd		The 53rd Infantry Brigade 18th Division took over the front covered by the Brigade. 2/Lieut. R.C. Cook M.C. trans.ferred to 58 Divisional Trench Mortars. 2/Lieut. W.T. KING joined the Brigade and was posted to C/290. Brig. General C.M. ROSS-JOHNSON C.B. C.M.G. D.S.O. G.O.C.R.A. III. Corps. visited all Battery positions.	
	3rd		Advance parties of Headquarters and all Batteries of the 169th Army Brigade R.F.A. came up to see the front own Battery positions. O.C. 169th Brigade spending the night at Brigade Headquarters.	
	6th		2/Lieut. J.L. HADFIELD and 2/Lieut. P.F. MUMFORD joined the Brigade and were posted to B/290 and A/290 respectively.	

Sheet II

Army Form C. 2118.

WAR DIARY
or
INTELLIGENCE SUMMARY.
(Erase heading not required.)

Place	Date	Hour	Summary of Events and Information	Remarks and references to Appendices
	1916			
June	7th		169th Army Brigade R.F.A. relieved 16 Brigade in action. Headquarters and Batteries moved to their Wagon lines at BAVELINCOURT.	
	9th		Brigade proceeded by route march and occupied billets at ARQUÈVES 4 miles WEST of AMIENS. On arrival in this area the 58th Division came under the XIIth Corps.	
	10th		"D" Battery returned from its school at AILLY-LE-SEC and rejoined the Brigade.	
	10th–12th		Batteries and Battery Staffs trained in mounted work with a view to prevent up skill and movement. A certain number of officers sent out almost daily to reconnoitre the neighbouring front of the Australian Corps and 31st French Corps, NORTH and SOUTH of AMIENS respectively in case the Division was required for reinforcing either of these fronts.	
	16th		Colonel C.T.H. PHILLIPS joined the Brigade and was posted 2nd in command of 87/290.	

Sheet III

Army Form C. 2118.

WAR DIARY
or
INTELLIGENCE SUMMARY.
(Erase heading not required.)

Place	Date	Hour	Summary of Events and Information	Remarks and references to Appendices
June	1916 19th		Brigade proceeded by route march and occupied wagon lines at BAVELINCOURT relieving 16 1st III Corps.	
	20th		Brigade relieved the 236th Brigade 47th Division in the line. Headquarters being established in the Quarry at D.4.c.2.4. Lt Colonel W.A.F. JONES D.S.O. taking over the line with the 4 Batteries of the Brigade and the 377th Battery 169th Army Brigade R.F.A. covering the front held by the 173rd Infantry Brigade astride the ALBERT–AMIENS ROAD. The daily allotment of ammunition being 1000 rounds 18 pdrs and 200 rounds 4.5 Hows for the Group. Major General F.W. RAMSAY C.M.G. D.S.O. G.O.C. 5th Division inspected Battery positions accompanied by the C.R.A.	
	23rd		Position of 377th Battery shelled by 5.9 Battery position wounding 1 officer and disabling 1 gun.	
	24		H.2. Battery consistently shelled vicinity of	

WAR DIARY
or
INTELLIGENCE SUMMARY.
(Erase heading not required.)

Army Form C. 2118.

Place: Sheet IV

Date	Hour	Summary of Events and Information	Remarks and references to Appendices
1918 June 24.		A/290 and B/290 positions firing about 300 rounds, 1 gun of B/290 receiving one or more direct hits, the gun being destroyed and 1 O.R. wounded.	
27th		Lieut: J. RADFORD-NORCOP joined the Divisional Artillery as Horse Officer 58th Divisional Artillery and was attached to this Brigade.	
June 1st		The following awards were made:-	
		MILITARY CROSS	
		2/Lieut: T. DUNN.	
		Lieut: (A/Major) F.C. MOORE.	
		DISTINGUISHED CONDUCT MEDAL	
		925409 Sergeant STEELE E.E.	
2nd		926310 B.S.M. GOOD S.H.	

W.D. Jones
Lt: Col: D.S.O.,
Comdg: 290th Brigade, R.F.A.

W.D. Jones
Lt: Col: D.S.O.,
Comdg: 290th Brigade, R.F.A.

WAR DIARY
290 Brigade R.F.A.
INTELLIGENCE SUMMARY

Vol 19

Army Form C. 2118.

Place	Date	Hour	Summary of Events and Information	Remarks and references to Appendices
	July 1st		On the night of June 30th/July 1st all batteries of the Group fired a barrage in connection with an operation by the 12th and 18th Divisions on our Left.	
	"	4ᵃ	In the early morning of the 4th all Batteries of the Group fired a barrage in conjunction with an attack by the Australian Corps on our right.	
	"	8ᵃ	At 9 pm received the order Battle Stations Practice	
	"	10ᵃ	377th Battery was relieved by B/108 Battery R.F.A.	
	"	12ᵈ	Lt Colonel W.A.F. JONES D.S.O. proceeded on 14 days leave to England. Major T.C. BECKHAM M.C. assumed command of the Group.	
	"	18ᵈ	2/Lieut F.G. THOMPSON was transferred to 58th Division Trench Mortars	
	"	20ᵈ	2/Lieut A.A. HARRIS joined the Brigade and was posted to "C" Battery	
	"	25ᵈ	All Batteries of the Group fired a barrage from 10 am. to 12 noon while a daylight raid was carried out by the Infantry.	
	"	26ᵈ	58th Divisional Zone was moved slightly to the right.	

WAR DIARY
or
INTELLIGENCE SUMMARY.
(Erase heading not required.)

Army Form C. 2118.

Place	Date	Hour	Summary of Events and Information	Remarks and references to Appendices
	July 26th		being reconstructed into two Groups. Right Group consisting of 5th Army Brigade R.F.A. B/86 Bde R.F.A. and B/86 Bde R.F.A. Left Group consisting of the 291st Brigade R.F.A. and its Brigade as a sub-group. All Batteries remained in their present position. Brigade Headquarters moving to D.A.D. 78.52.	
	29th		Lieut. C.W.D. Jones was transferred to X.II Corps R.A. The allotment of ammunition throughout the month for harassing fire was 400 rounds for 18-pdrs and 75 rounds for 4.5" Howitzers for Group.	

J. Kepton
Major M.C.
for Lt. Colonel
Commanding 290 Brigade R.F.A.

58th Divl. Artillery

290th BRIGADE, R. F. A.

AUGUST 1918.

Army Form C. 2118.

WAR DIARY
200 Brigade R.H.A
INTELLIGENCE SUMMARY.
(Erase heading not required.)

Place	Date	Hour	Summary of Events and Information	Remarks and references to Appendices
	July 3rd		Lt. Colonel Witt, June D.S.O. returned from 10 days leave to England. During the night of 3rd July/4th August and 14th/15th August the Brigade was relieved in the line by the 25th Divisional Artillery. The Brigade proceeded to Wagon Lines at BAZENCOURT.	
August	2nd		Brigade and Battery Commanders proceded by bus to reconnoitre positions in the neighbourhood of WELCOME WOOD. Capt. C.H. Phillips was wounded and struck off strength.	
"	3rd		Reconnaissance continued and in the evening Batteries commenced to dump ammunition at the Battery positions at 6.0 p.m. per gun.	
"	4th		Capt. G.R. Johnston joined. The Brigade and was posted to Command of B/290.	
"	6		Owing to an enemy raid penetrating to the positions allotted, fresh positions had to be allotted for C/290 and B/290.	
"	7th		Brigade Headquarters moved to Batt. Headquarters at T.22.d.2.4 with 174 Inf/Bde. all the Batteries coming into action in the evening.	
"	8th		Barrage fire at 4.20 a.m. in conjunction with an Infantry attack. All Batteries advanced to forward positions in the evening. Headquarters being	

Army Form C. 2118.

WAR DIARY
290 Brigade R.F.A.
INTELLIGENCE SUMMARY.
(Erase heading not required.)

Sheet 1 - II

Instructions regarding War Diaries and Intelligence Summaries are contained in F.S. Regs., Part II. and the Staff Manual respectively. Title pages will be prepared in manuscript.

Place	Date	Hour	Summary of Events and Information	Remarks and references to Appendices
August	8th (cont)		Transferred to K.31.c.90.35.	
"	9th		Barrage fired at 5.30 p.m. in conjunction with an infantry attack.	
			A/290 and D/290 moved to more advanced positions in the evening.	
"	10th		Brigade came under the command of the 4th Australian Divl Artillery.	
			A/290 and D/290 moved to more advanced positions.	
"	11th		Brigade Headquarters moved to K.27.c.7.9.	
"	13th		Brigade again came under orders of 58th D.A. forming part of	
			the "Liaison Force". All Batteries moved to more forward positions	
"	20th		The "Liaison Force" ceased to exist and Bde came under Orders of 4 Aus. Div Art.	
"	22nd		At 4.45 a.m. Barrage fires in connection with an attack by the	
			47th Division on the Left.	
"	24th		Barrage fires at 1 a.m. and BRAY sur SOMME was captured by Australian left.	
			The Batteries moved forward during the day and Headquarters moved	
			to K.35.a.6.3.	
"	25		Barrage fires at 5 a.m. in support of a further attack by the	
			Infantry. Later in the day Batteries moved to positions in	

Army Form C. 2118.

Sheet III

WAR DIARY
290 Brigade R.F.A
INTELLIGENCE SUMMARY.
(Erase heading not required.)

Place	Date	Hour	Summary of Events and Information	Remarks and references to Appendices
August	25th (cont)		the neighbourhood of B.R.A.T. Headquarters to L.14.a.8.3.	
"	27th		2/Lieut J.M. MASHALL joined the Brigade and was posted to B290. All Batteries moved to positions in the neighbourhood of BILLON WOOD. Headquarters being at F.28.6.6.8. Brigade came under orders of the 58th Div. Arty.	
"	28th		At 4.45 am a barrage was fired in conjunction with an attack by the 58th Divisional Infantry.	
"	29th		All Batteries moved forward. Headquarters being established in Quarries A.30.6.8.3.	
"	30th		All Batteries occupied positions in front of MARRIERS WOOD with Headqrs at B.27.6.40.	
"	31st		At 5.10 am Barrage fired in connection with an attack on MARRIERS WOOD which was taken by our Infantry	

M. Matthews Lt Col
Comdg 290 Bde R.F.A

290 Bde R.F.A.
Vol 21

WAR DIARY
or
INTELLIGENCE SUMMARY

Army Form C. 2118.

Place	Date	Hour	Summary of Events and Information	Remarks and references to Appendices
SEPTEMBER	1.		On the night Aug 31/Sept 1st "A" "B" & "D" Batteries moved to new advanced positions. At 5.30 am a barrage was fired in conjunction with an infantry attack on BOUCHAVESNES, which was captured.	
	2.		The enemy Headquarters and batteries moved forward. Convoy under orders of the 74th (Yeomanry) Division and forming liaison with the 229 Infantry Brigade.	
			A barrage was fired at 5.30 am supporting an attack on MOISLAINS. The Infantry took the village but eventually had to fall back practically to their start line.	
	3		Wire C.M. Legacy repaired the Brigade and was posted to A/Hqr.	
	4		MOISLAINS was found to be evacuated, and positions were occupied W. of the CANAL DU NORD.	
	5		The enemy having withdrawn the Brigade advanced and bivouacked for the night on the W. side of the CANAL DU NORD near MOISLAINS.	
	6		The Brigade advanced in close support of the Infantry	

WAR DIARY
or
INTELLIGENCE SUMMARY.
(Erase heading not required.)

Army Form C. 2118.

Place	Date	Hour	Summary of Events and Information	Remarks and references to Appendices
	7		during the days and in the evening advanced halts. Came under the command of the 55th D.A., and occupied positions near GURLU WOOD, Division being performed with the 175th Infantry Brigade.	
	8		The Battern again moved forward. Headquarters moved to AIZECOURT-LE-BAS in liaison with the 175th Infantry Brigade. Headquarters moved at 6 am to the 2/Lt attn knocks unitate. North of LIERAMONT, west of LIERAMONT. A barrage was fired supporting the attack of the 174th Infantry Brigade on EPEHY. The attack was successful but during the day the Infantry were compelled to withdraw to their original start line.	
	9		In the afternoon Brigade Headquarters moved to LIERAMONT back in liaison with the 173rd Infantry Brigade.	
	10		The attack on EPEHY and PEZIERES was resumed, the battery firing a barrage in support of the 173rd Brigade. The Infantry again captured their objective, and were again forced	

WAR DIARY
or
INTELLIGENCE SUMMARY.
(Erase heading not required.)

Army Form C. 2118.

Place	Date	Hour	Summary of Events and Information	Remarks and references to Appendices
	13		back to their about line. 2/Lt. G.C. WOOLVER went out with an opened patrol, and hostile to his activity returning was presumed a prisoner of war.	
	14		W. K.A.R. Strottmann joined the Brigade and was posted to C/290. New battery position were reconnoitred E. of VILLERS FAUCON and W. of EPEHY. The Brigade came under the orders of the 184th D.A.	
	17		Headquarters moved to the E. of VILLERS FAUCON, batteries to the position reconnoitred on the 14th.	
	18		The Brigade supported an attack designed to capture EPEHY, PEZIERES and RONSSOY, and to draw the enemy back on to the Hindenburg line. EPEHY, PEZIERES and RONSSOY were taken but the enemy here remained a short distance W. of the Hindenburg line. 2/Lt. E.V. STALEY was killed, and LIEUT. T. VESEY STRONG was gassed and sent to hospital.	
	19		All batteries moved in the early morning to positions W. of RONSSOY. Headquarters were established at ST EMILIE	

Army Form C. 2118.

WAR DIARY
or
INTELLIGENCE SUMMARY.
(Erase heading not required.)

Instructions regarding War Diaries and Intelligence Summaries are contained in F. S. Regs., Part II. and the Staff Manual respectively. Title pages will be prepared in manuscript.

Place	Date	Hour	Summary of Events and Information	Remarks and references to Appendices
	20		Several local attacks made with artillery support but little progress was very slow. Much harassing fire was carried out by day and night.	
	21			
	22			
	24		"B" Battery was back 200 yards further west of Ronssoy, their previous position being constantly and heavily shelled.	
	25		Him to aid the 27th American Division took over the front. The Artillery under the CRA 4th Australian Division, who reorganised and consisting of the 110th 290th & 29th Brigades RFA. Lt Col W.A.F. Jones DSO took command of the Centre Group.	
	26		At 9.30 pm the preparatory 48-hours bombardment for a general attack on the Hindenburg line began. A special fire concentration fired by 18 pdrs	
	27		At 5.30 am the 27th American Division attacked & gain the Knoll ridge line for the Hn. main attack. Run objective was gained and prisoners taken, but our own infantry by evening were forced back to their original line. Centre Group co-operated. D/290 who heavily shelled with the enemy morning and 2/Lt Robinson killed. Wire cutting commenced	

WAR DIARY or INTELLIGENCE SUMMARY

Army Form C. 2118.

Place	Date	Hour	Summary of Events and Information	Remarks and references to Appendices
	28		Patrols were reconnoitred E. of RONSSOY and occupied at dusk. Brigade Headquarters moved to RONSSOY.	
	29	5.30 am	The Centre Group fired a creeping barrage supporting the attack of the 27th American Division on the Hindenburg Line. The Hindenburg Line was captured and LE CATELET, but during the day was never in our actual fighting. The front line at night was immediately E. of the CANAL DE ST QUENTIN.	
	30	1.30 am	The 110th, 290th and 291st Brigades came under the command of C.R.A. 3rd Aus. Division. The 110th Brigade Ryg. left the CENTRE GROUP. The "tipping up" of the Hindenburg Line was commenced.	
			The Military Medal was awarded to the following N.C.Os and men. (5th ARO. No. 512 dated 18.9.18.)	
			926454 Sgt. J.A. LLOYD A/290	
			925719 Corp. A.T. POTTER B/290	
			97316 Gunner T. TODD C/290	
			287916 Gunner J.A.R.S. STEVENSON C/290	
			92582 Driver H. HODGSON A/290.	
			406271 Serjm. G. SCOTT-CORMACK R.E. att'd H.Q. 290th Brigade R.F.A.	

W.D. Jones
Lt Col.
C/S 290th Bde R.F.A.

Army Form C. 2118.

WAR DIARY
or
INTELLIGENCE SUMMARY.
(Erase heading not required.)

Instructions regarding War Diaries and Intelligence Summaries are contained in F. S. Regs., Part II. and the Staff Manual respectively. Title pages will be prepared in manuscript.

Place	Date	Hour	Summary of Events and Information	Remarks and references to Appendices
October.	1st.		Mopping up along the HINDENBURG LINE continued. Artillery re-grouped, the Brigade forming part of the RIGHT GROUP under Lt. Colonel W.G.ALLSOP D.S.O., Commanding 8th Australian Field Artillery Brigade, covering 11th Australian Infantry Brigade.	
	2nd.		Headquarters and Batteries moved to positions W. of BONY.	
	3rd.		At 6.5 a.m. an attack was made under a creeping barrage to capture the RED LINE including LE CATELET - GOUY - and PROSPECT HILL. These objectives were taken but by the evening the Infantry were forced back to the top of PROSPECT HILL and the Southern portion of LE CATELET and GOUY.	
	4th.		LE CATELET retaken. N.E. portion was lost, later under a counter attack, under direct orders of the 113th Infantry Bde, 38th Division.	
	5th.		Headquarters and Batteries moved to N.W. of LE CATELET. (The Bosch having fallen back during the night).	
	6th.		Headquarters and Batteries moved to positions S. of GOUY re-joining the 18th Divisional Artillery. Headquarters at MONT ST. MARTIN.	
	8th.		Attack was made to capture SERAIN and VILLERS OUTREAUX which was successful. A large number of civilians were released in SERAIN and Villages East.	
	9th.		Headquarters and Batteries came out of action and marched to AIZECOURT le BAS Area.	
	11th.		Headquarters and Batteries at intervals marched to TINCOURT and entrained.	
	12/13th.		The Brigade detrained and went into billets at HERSIN coming under VIIIth Corps 1st Army.	
	13h/18th.		Brigade remained at HERSIN.	
			18th/	

Army Form C. 2118.

WAR DIARY
or
INTELLIGENCE SUMMARY.
(Erase heading not required.)

Place	Date	Hour	Summary of Events and Information	Remarks and references to Appendices
October.	18th.		Brigade proceeded by road to HARNES. Coming under the 1st Corps Fifth Army as Divisional Reserve, the Division attacking with little or no opposition in the advance meeting	
	19th.		Brigade proceeded to RUE DE MONCHEAUX.	
	20th.		Brigade proceeded to VERT BOIS area.	
	21st.		Brigade proceeded to AIX.	
	21/27th.		Brigade remained at AIX in Corps Reserve.	
	27th.		Brigade relieved the 291st Brigade R.F.A. in the Line, coming under orders of the Brigadier General 174th Infantry Brigade, with Brigade Headquarters at RONGY.	
	27/31st.		The Line remained practically stationary on the banks of the SCHELDT being held strongly by the enemy with Machine guns.	
			HONOURS AND AWARDS.	
			THE MILITARY CROSS.	
			2/Lt. W.T.KING. C/290th Bde. RFA.	
			2/Lt. L.F.ROBINSON. D/290th Bde. RFA.	
			(Since Killed in Action).	
			THE MILITARY MEDAL.	
			925636. Farr. Sergt. C.F.COOPER. B/290th RFA.	
			926446. Cpl. Whlr. S.T.TOMLINSON. B/290th RFA.	
			690181. Driver. A. HOYTON. D/290th RFA.	
			926265. Driver. C. KERRIDGE. D/290th RFA.	

Army Form C. 2118.

WAR DIARY
or
INTELLIGENCE SUMMARY.
(Erase heading not required.)

Summary of Events and Information

THE MILITARY MEDAL. (Contd).

926233.	Driver.	E. FATHERS.	D/290th Bde RFA.
690318.	Driver.	J. ASHCROFT.	D/290th Bde RFA.
17128.	Sergt.	H. STAITE.	C/290th Bde RFA.
925538.	Sergt.	W.G. BAKER.	C/290th Bde RFA.
685171.	Sergt.	J. FORSHAW.	B/290th Bde. RFA.
191251.	Gunner.	J. SPENCE.	B/290th Bde RFA.

..................Lt.Colonel. D.S.O.
Commanding,
290th BRIGADE R. F. A.

Army Form C. 2118.

WAR DIARY
or
INTELLIGENCE SUMMARY.
(Erase heading not required.)

Instructions regarding War Diaries and Intelligence Summaries are contained in F.S. Regs., Part II. and the Staff Manual respectively. Title pages will be prepared in manuscript.

Place	Date	Hour	Summary of Events and Information	Remarks and references to Appendices
November	1st		The 174th Infantry Brigade with one battalion of the 173rd attached took over the defence of the whole Divisional Front covered by the 290th Brigade with B/242 and D/242 attached under the command of Lt. Colonel W.A.F.JONES D.S.O.	
	1/7th.		Preparations were made for an attack to take place on the Divisional Front on or about the 9th.	
	7/8th.		The enemy retired during the night.	
	9th.		In conjunction with the 174th Infantry Brigade took up the pursuit of the enemy and advanced during the day as far as PONT DE CALLENELLE.	
	10th.		Continued the pursuit as far as BELOEIL receiving a great reception from the civilians in the various villages.	
	11th.		Brigade marched to GROSAGE, news being received just as the Brigade moved off that the Armistice had been signed and that hostilities would cease at 11 a.m.	
	11/17th.		Brigade remained in billets at GROSAGE.	
	14th.		A Thanksgiving Service was held by the 174th Infantry Brigade at which a representative party of the Brigade were present.	
	17th.		Brigade moved to more comfortable billets, Headquarters, B/290 and C/290 being at QUEVAUCAMPS, A/290 and D/290 at BLATON.	
	18/30th.		Brigade remained in billets, the mornings being spent in drill and training, the afternoons in Football and Sports with classes for Education in the evenings.	

HONOURS AND AWARDS.

THE MILITARY CROSS.

Capt. V. BANHAM, C.F.   Attd. 290th Brigade R.F.A.

..........Lt.Colonel D.S.O.
Commanding
290th Brigade R. F. A.

Army Form C. 2118.

WAR DIARY
or
INTELLIGENCE SUMMARY.
(Erase heading not required.)

Instructions regarding War Diaries and Intelligence Summaries are contained in F. S. Regs., Part II. and the Staff Manual respectively. Title pages will be prepared in manuscript.

December 1918.

Place	Date	Hour	Summary of Events and Information	Remarks and references to Appendices
QUEVAUCAMPS	Dec 1.		Lt. Col. W.A.F. Jones D.S.O. proceeded to ENGLAND on 14 days leave, and a six weeks Senior Officers' Tactical Course at CAMBRIDGE.	
	Dec 2.		The 58th Division was inspected by General Sir H.S. HORNE K.C.B. K.C.M.G. Commanding First Army. The inspection concluded with a march past.	
	Dec 5.		His Majesty King George V visited the Divisional Area, passing through GRANDGLISE and BASECLES. Large numbers of men gathered in groups along the road to cheer His Majesty as he passed.	

J. Salmon
Major
Cmdg. 290th Brigade R.F.A.

WAR DIARY
290th BRIGADE R.F.A. 58 DIV
INTELLIGENCE SUMMARY

Army Form C. 2118.

Place	Date	Hour	Summary of Events and Information	Remarks and references to Appendices
QUEVAUCAMPS	MARCH 1919 8.3.19		Owing to the progress of Demobilization around LEUZE at the beginning of March. Accordingly QUEVAUCAMPS was occupied by the 290th Brigade R.F.A. on the 8th March, Headquarters "A" and "D" Batteries moving to BLICQUY, "B" and "C" Batteries to AUBECHIES. Demobilization proceeded during the month.	

W. D. Jones.
Lieutenant Colonel.
Commanding
290th Brigade R.F.A.

WO 95/2995/3

58 Division Troops

291 BDE RFA
(Formerly 2/2 London BDE)

1915 OCT — 1916 FEB

Box 2995

2860

Army Form C. 2118.

2/1 Bde RFA (formerly 2/2 Lon Bde) 7/2 Bde RFA

WAR DIARY or INTELLIGENCE SUMMARY.

(Erase heading not required.)

Instructions regarding War Diaries and Intelligence Summaries are contained in F. S. Regs., Part II. and the Staff Manual respectively. Title pages will be prepared in manuscript.

COMMDG. 2/2nd LONDON BAGDE R.F.A.
[signature] BREVET COL.

Place	Date	Hour	Summary of Events and Information	Remarks and references to Appendices
	1915 Oct			
	4.			
SAXMUNDHAM	10.	11.30 p.m.	Notification received "Usual air Craft positions will be taken up at once"	
	15.		All lights extinguished - Two guns in pits manned and prepared for action -	
	5.			
	10.15	1 am	Order received to resume normal working. -	
	13.			
SAXMUNDHAM	10.15	8.0pm	Message received "Anti air craft intelligence and observation posts will be taken up at once"	
			All lights extinguished - Two guns in pits manned and prepared for action.	
		11.20 p.m.	Two explosions heard in S.W. direction.	
		11.45 p.m.	Engines of an Air Ship distinctly heard - apparently proceeding in a N.Easterly direction. after 10 minutes sound ceased.	
	14.	1.30 A.M.	Engines of two Air ships heard - One apparently travelling in a N.Easterly direction and the other in an Easterly direction from the W.	
	10.15		Guns again manned and prepared for action - After about 20 minutes sound ceased.	
		2.30am	Slight noise of Air ship heard - but soon died away. -	
	19.			
SAXMUNDHAM	10.15	10.45 a.m.	Message received "Zepplin has been sighted 70 miles due E of SOUTHWOLD"	
			Two guns with trails dug in were manned in HURTS HALL PARK.	
			Two " " " " " in KNODISHALL WHIN	
			Three " " " " " in HAZLEWOOD COMMON	
			No Zeppelin sighted nor heard.	

2353 Wt. W2544/1454 700,000 5/15 D. D. & L. A.D.S.S. Forms/C 2118.

Army Form C. 2118.

WAR DIARY
or
INTELLIGENCE SUMMARY.

(Erase heading not required.)

Instructions regarding War Diaries and Intelligence Summaries are contained in F. S. Regs., Part II. and the Staff Manual respectively. Title pages will be prepared in manuscript.

Place	Date	Hour	Summary of Events and Information	Remarks and references to Appendices
WOODBRIDGE	20. 10. 15.	8.45 pm.	Message received "Stand by"	
		9.25 pm.	" " "Take up usual outposts - Zeppelins reported over the WASH and the THAMES. Two Guns were run out to meadow adjoining BARRACK FARM - trails dug in and prepared for action.	
		12.00 midnight	Message received "Resume normal working"	

W. Mitchell

Brevet Colonel,
Commanding, 2/2nd London Brigade, R.F.A.
Woodbridge,
31/10/15.

Army Form C. 2118.

WAR DIARY
INTELLIGENCE SUMMARY.
(Erase heading not required.)

Place	Date	Hour	Summary of Events and Information	Remarks and references to Appendices
WOODBRIDGE.	11/11/15	6. p.m.	6th. County of London Battery arrived from TADWORTH & went into billets.	

W.C. Nicholls
BREVET COLONEL
Commanding 2/2nd LONDON BRIGADE R.F.A.

Army Form C. 2118.

WAR DIARY
or
INTELLIGENCE SUMMARY.
(Erase heading not required.)

Place	Date	Hour	Summary of Events and Information	Remarks and references to Appendices
WOODBRIDGE	7/12/15		Inspection by Lieut General R.C. Broadwood C.B. Commanding 1st Army on BRIGHTWELL HEATH	
	13/12/15		Inspection by Major General J.M. Brunker Inspector of R.H. & R.F.A. on BRIGHTWELL HEATH	
	29/12/15		Inspection by Brigadier General E.J. Cooper C.B. M.V.O. D.S.O. Commanding 58th (London) Division on MARTLESHAM HEATH	

Wm. Nicholls
BREVET COLONEL
COMMDG. 2/2nd LONDON BRIGADE R.F.A.

2/5th Lalo. Brigade R.F.A.

Army Form C. 2118

WAR DIARY
or
INTELLIGENCE SUMMARY

(Erase heading not required.)

Instructions regarding War Diaries and Intelligence Summaries are contained in F.S. Regs., Part II. and the Staff Manual respectively. Title Pages will be prepared in manuscript.

Place	Date	Hour	Summary of Events and Information	Remarks and references to Appendices
WOODBRIDGE	17.1.16	10.30 A.M.	Fair 15°F. March I B.L.C. Gun, 4 Ammunition Wagons, 105 Horses, 2 Officers & 87 N.C.O.s & Men of the 2/6th Battery – & 4 S.S. Wagons, 18 Mules & 10 N.C.O.s & Men of the single Ammunition Column proceeded to ORFORD to help R.F.C.	

R.T. Green, Lt Col.
Comdg. 2/5th Lalo Brigade R.F.A.

Army Form C. 2118.

WAR DIARY

~~INTELLIGENCE SUMMARY~~

(Erase heading not required.)

Instructions regarding War Diaries and Intelligence Summaries are contained in F. S. Regs., Part II. and the Staff Manual respectively. Title pages will be prepared in manuscript.

Place	Date	Hour	Summary of Events and Information	Remarks and references to Appendices
WOODBRIDGE	1916 FEB			
	6.			
	2.			
	16.	1 pm.	2 Officers, 87 N.C.O's & Men, and 103 horses of the 2/6th Battery - 3 G.S. Wagons, 16 Mules and 10 N.C.O's & Men of the Brigade Ammunition Column arrived from O R F O R D on completion of duty as Depot Battery.	

R.F.Fizza
Brevet Colonel,
Commanding, 2/2nd London Brigade, R.F.A.(T.F.)

WO 95/2995/4

B E F

58. DIVISION TROOPS

291 BRIGADE R.F.A.
(FORMERLY 2/2 LONDON BDE TO MAY 1916)

1917 JAN — 1919 MAY

Box 2905

WAR DIARY Vol 19

291st Bde RFA

WAR DIARY 1/3rd W. Brigade R.F.A.

INTELLIGENCE SUMMARY

Army Form C. 2118.

Instructions regarding War Diaries and Intelligence Summaries are contained in F.S. Regs., Part II. and the Staff Manual respectively. Title pages will be prepared in manuscript.

Place	Date	Hour	Summary of Events and Information	Remarks and references to Appendices
HEYTESBURY	22/1/17	2.30 p	Left for Southampton	WW
SOUTHAMPTON	22/1/17	7 pm	Completed embarkation and sailed in S/S Archimedes for HAVRE	WW
HAVRE	23/1/17	9.30 am	Arrived at HAVRE and disembarked, then marched to No 2 Rest Camp	WW
"	"			WW
"	24/1/17 9.17		Entrained and left ABBEVILLE due here 7am 25/1/17 pm	WW
ABBEVILLE	25/1/17	5.35 pm	Arrived ABBEVILLE 10½ hours late & received instructions to proceed to AUXI le CHATEAU	WW
"	—		Convoy AUXI le CHATEAU at 11.50 pm 25/1/17, detrained and received orders to march to WAVANS and billet	WW
WAVANS	26/1/17		Marched for LUCHEUX at 8.45 am arriving 2 pm. En route received instructions as to reorganization of Divisional Artillery by which D/291st Battery received a section of 4.5 Hows and Captain Sauze from D/293 Battery which was broken up. Captain Sauze reported with his section	WW
LUCHEUX	6/2/17		Transfer of section as above completed	WW
"	10/2/17		Major G. Antelhems K.O. and † file transfer from each Battery effect gone	WW

WAR DIARY of 74th Brigade R.F.A.

Army Form C. 2118.

INTELLIGENCE SUMMARY.

Place	Date	Hour	Summary of Events and Information	Remarks and references to Appendices
LUCHEUX	10/2/17	—	A, B, "D" Batteries being attached to 48th Brigade R.F.A. while C Battery was attached to 246th Brigade R.F.A. at BAILLEUMONT. at BEAUMETZ.	[initials]
LUCHEUX	13/2/17	—	While the Brigade was at NAVANS 4 horses (over) died from of which died of contagious pleuro-pneumonia caught either on the front or train. The other three were kept or being cases brought about by the extremes of temperature from front to No 2 Rest camp at NAVANS where the night temperature was down to 17°FAHR. and then two trains to freight lines in the open or shelters, the night at NAVANS there was a temperature of 9°FAH. No further cases have occurred to date.	[initials]
LUCHEUX	18/2/17	—	Personal of A, B & D Batteries transferred from 48th Brigade R.F.A. to 246th Brigade R.F.A. and were attached to A,C,& D Batteries respectively these being the Batteries which they were to relieve	[initials]
BAILLEUMONT	21/2/17		A, B, "C" Batteries sent in one section of personnel to take over from A,C,& D Batteries respectively of 246th Brigade R.F.A. [strikethrough] being instructed [/strikethrough] as guns in the Pits. "D" Battery sent in one section	

3.

Army Form C. 2118.

WAR DIARY H.Q. 291st Brigade R.F.A.
or
INTELLIGENCE SUMMARY.
(Erase heading not required.)

Place	Date	Hour	Summary of Events and Information	Remarks and references to Appendices

Hours {"D" 246th Brig. removing two of their guns (How) RFA.
complete with {guns}

[signature]
Lt. Col.
Comdg. 291st Brigade R.F.A.

WAR DIARY of 291st Brigade R.F.A.
or
INTELLIGENCE SUMMARY.
(Erase heading not required.)

Army Form C. 2118.

Place	Date	Hour	Summary of Events and Information	Remarks and references to Appendices
BAILLEULMONT	25/8/17		A.B.C Batteries took over guns complete from the Batteries of 246th Brigade. "A" from "A", "B" from "C", "C" taking over "B" Battery respectively. "D" Battery completed their relief, taking their own guns & tm.	
"	26/8/17		The 291st Brigade H.Qrs relieved the 246th Brigade H.Qrs at 10.30 a.m. the relief of Batteries having been reported complete by that time and all 246th Brigade personnel clear.	
"	6/9/17		Small raid by Cmele on our trenches at the foot of LIMERICK LANE in C.2.B.	
"	25/8/17		The Raid being retired from our front. "B" Battery 291st Brigade tog-	
"	27/8/17		ethered to more forward support. Infantry from F.14 Central to B & Wireless BOIRY BECQUERELLE (Reference map 51C SW. 20000). The Battery being placed in Appendix 2 under Lt Col H.N. Clark. Comdg 290 Bde R.F.A. H.Qs with B.C. "D" Battery moved to ADINFER WOOD (THE LODGE)	

Morley
Lt Col
Comdg 291st Brigade R.F.A.

SECRET.

COPY No. 11

OPERATION ORDERS No. 5.
BY
LIEUT-COLONEL W.T. ODAM
COMMANDING, 291st., BDE., RFA.

----

1.   The NORTHERN BOUNDARY of 58th DIVISION is BOIRY BECQUERELLE - BOISLEUX AU MONT - FISHEUX all inclusive.
The SOUTHERN BOUNDARY of 58th DIVISION ADINFER- ST LEGER - CROISELLE all exclusive.

The 173rd Infantry Brigade will hold line from BOIRY BECQUERELLE inclusive along road through T.14.b. to ST. LEGER MILL at T.21.d.9.1

The 30th DIVISION has relieved the 175th Infantry Brigade north of BOIRY BACQUERELLE.

2. A/291st., Brigade, R.F.A. will relieve C/150th Brigade, and will support the left of 173rd Infantry Brigade from S 14 CENTRAL to BOIRY BACQUERELLE.

3. A/291st., Bde., R.F.A. will march at 8.30 a.m. on the morning of 20th March. The Battery Commander will go forward at once and reconnoitre for a position to cover frontage as in para 2 of these orders. The Battery Commander will get in touch with the Infantry Battalion Commander, and establish a close Liason with him.

4. Suggested position for Wagon Lines HENDECOURT or ADINFER.

5. Great care must be exercised in occupation of position, if really necessary, this will not be carried out until after dusk, but with careful leading the occupation may be able to be carried out in day light.

6. Brigade Headquarters will remain at BAILLEULMONT, where reports will be sent.

7. Please acknowledge.

LIEUT - COLONEL,
COMMANDING, 291st., BRIGADE, R.F.A.

Bde., Hdqrs.,
19.3.17.
Issued at 10.30 pm.

No. 1 copy to C.R.A. by Orderly.
 " 2 "   " 173rd Infantry Bde.,   by Orderly.
 " 3 "   " 174th Infantry Bde.,   "   "
 " 4 "   " 175th Infantry Bde.,   "   "
 " 5 "   " "A" Battery - 291st.Bde.,"   "
 " 6 "   " "B"   -   "   "   "
 " 7 "   " "C"   -   "   "   "
 " 8 "   " "D"   -   "   "   "
 " 9 - 12 FILED.

B/
58th

Army Form C. 2118.

War Diary 93rd Brigade RHA Vol 4

WAR DIARY
or
INTELLIGENCE SUMMARY.
(Erase heading not required.)

Place	Date	Hour	Summary of Events and Information	Remarks and references to Appendices
ADINFER	27/3		Head Quarters and B.C.D. Batteries moved from BAILLEULMONT to ADINFER. H.Q. in the road and the Batteries in vicinity of ADINFER.	PP
MOYENVILLE	25/3		Brig. H.Q. moved in evening 27th Aug. B Battery occupied a position in outskirts of HAMELINCOURT. "D" Battery behind a railway embankment close to MOYENVILLE. C Battery remained at ADINFER which was the Brigade magazine line.	PP B PP
-,-	29/3		58th Divisional Artillery attached to 21st Divisional Artillery for operations pending. The 93rd Brigade forming a sub-group under Lt Col Fitzgerald commanding 95th Brigade RHA. See O.O. no 33	PP
-,-	30/3		B & C Batteries moved up & occupied positions in vicinity of ST LEGER to support attack on CROISILLES	
BULECOURT? 7.25 & 77 May 5/A SW	Apl 2	5.15am	Moved to Battle H.Q. for the attack. (Battle H.Q. 7.25 & 77 May 5/A SW) 515am Barrage opened and by 7.30 attack was reported as successful. Orders for operations attached, also Order of the day of G.O.C. 5 Army, and Copy of 3rd Division Scheme commanding the — 31st Division.	PP
MOYENVILLE Apl 5	Apl 5		C & D Batteries moved to new positions near ST LEGER and preparations commenced for operations on a larger scale.	PP

WAR DIARY 2nd Bridge R.N.A.
or
INTELLIGENCE SUMMARY

Army Form C. 2118

Place	Date	Hour	Summary of Events and Information	Remarks and references to Appendices
MOYENVILLE Apl 5			Bombardment of HINDENBURG LINE commenced at 7am	
	Apl 6		Moved to Batt. Hind Quarters at T 25 a 77 M/S S1 63w	
Batt.H.Q.	Apl 6		Batteries commenced bombardment	
"	Apl 7		Bombardment continued	
"	Apl 8		" 70	
"	Apl 9		" 50	
"	Apl 10		Z day. All Batteries fire a barrage. The attack succeeds at first, at the audacious Infantry have had no response.	
"	Apl 11		Further bombardment performed.	
"	Apl 12		Attack by Infantry to be repeated. No altar movement.	
"	Apl 13		Bombardment of enemy trenches continued.	
"	Apl 15		Attack by 112th Brigade by bending Eastwood Artillery established a trench some 300 yds further forward.	
			Were relieved by 13th Brigade RFA that Midday completed 2nd 11:35 pm. Bombardment returned by West Country 2 Fn. also CRA authority with all Batteries arrived at New way for way with instructions to reconnoitre for new positions for attack on SULLEN COURT. 2nd 58th Division	
ERVILLERS	4/14			

WAR DIARY

291st Brigade RFA

INTELLIGENCE SUMMARY

Army Form C. 2118

Place	Date	Hour	Summary of Events and Information	Remarks and references to Appendices
Battle HA. at B.17.B.36 Map 57C NW	15/4/17		Artillery being formed into one Group being called the 58th Divisional Group under Lt.Col.A.Clark. Battle HQrs established at B.17.B.3.6 close to Group Head Quarters. "A" Battery occupies position east of ECOUST ST MEIN the same enemy	
—	16/4/17		Enemy shelled the ECOUST valley vigorously early this morning. Enemy Cronalchin damage to material. Capt. Lance & 2/Lt. Johnston severely wounded and 2/Lt. A. Firth & 2/Lt. R.L. Conlund killed also 3 gunners killed and 5 wounded all belonging to "C" Battery. 2/Lt. H.T. Miles of D Battery was also wounded & 1 gunner killed & two wounded. Capt. J.G. Ferris & 2/Lt. H.S. Miles then 7 wounds. "C" Battery had 2 men killed and two wounded from enemy bombardment on this day. "C" Battery	
—	17/4/17		D Battery had 4 men wounded by enemy shell fire. Capt. Young assumed command temporarily.	
—	22/4/17		Position no changed. Capt. Drake assumed command temporarily.	
—	23/4/17		Capt. E.C. Young posted to command "A" Battery (291st Brigade) The effect of the terrible bad weather and extremely bad work the horses have to do in bringing up ammunition has resulted in 165 deaths & 321 evacuations to Mobile Veterinary sections. The Horses mostly have stood the abominable weather of the winter	

Army Form C. 2118.

WAR DIARY
or
INTELLIGENCE SUMMARY.
(Erase heading not required.)

Instructions regarding War Diaries and Intelligence Summaries are contained in F. S. Regs., Part II. and the Staff Manual respectively. Title pages will be prepared in manuscript.

Place	Date	Hour	Summary of Events and Information	Remarks and references to Appendices
			has been 12 lbs of oats instead of the 9 lbs which has been the ration from early July to March 23rd.	

Morley
Col
Comdg Sq? "D" Rough Riders
R.H.A.

Vol 5

CONFIDENTIAL
****

WAR DIARY

OF

201st Infy. Bde. H.Q.

From 3/5/17
To 21/5/17

WAR DIARY
or
INTELLIGENCE SUMMARY.
(Erase heading not required.)

Army Form C. 2118.

21st Brigade NW

Place	Date	Hour	Summary of Events and Information	Remarks and references to Appendices
Bullecourt at B17 & B6 May 5/C MW	3/5/17	2am 3.30	Supported the attack by (62nd Division) 185th Brigade on BULLECOURT which was unsuccessful although the front objectives were taken but lost again rather than two hours. Attacks continued but without success.	(A)
	4/5/17	3.45	Supported the attack of 20th Brigade (7th Division) on BULLECOURT which was a partial success, getting into village from EAST end. My first report.	(B) (C)
	5/5/17	11am	Attack renewed made further small gain	(D)
	5/5/17	12 noon	A third attack made but in the evening the Brigade (7th) were back in same position as on 7th inst	(E)
	6/5/17	7pm	A further attack made on BULLECOURT & an advance of a few yards held	(F)
	6/5/17	—	Supported attack of 91st Brigade who relieved 20th Bg but no further progress made	(G)
	7/5/17		Several more attacks made this day without success	(H)
	15/5/17		174th Inf Bgde Hqrs relieved 91st Bg. This brought 58th Divn Infantry into the line. Lt Cronny killed while F.O.O.	(I) (J)
	17/5/17	2am	2/5 Battln & 174 Inf Bgde attacked unsuccessfully & BULLECOURT was at last in our hands. Enemy held Trenches north of village	(K)

WAR DIARY
INTELLIGENCE SUMMARY

Army Form C. 2118.

27th Infantry Bde RM(T)

Place	Date	Hour	Summary of Events and Information	Remarks and references to Appendices
Bullecourt O.17.b.3.6	18/5/17		Lt E. Atkinson killed on his way to Observation station. A Barrage shot	(B)
"	21/5/17	3.45	2/6 Bttn & Col 2nd (94th Lt Infty) attacked BOVIS TRENCH. They attacked then objective, but owing to heavy enemy MG's shell holes &c with machine guns the Battalion was driven back to original line. Artillery good but I think if no artillery barrage had been used instead our strength up to 250 opto, the Infty by stealth might have been more successful, as the ground in front would have been more thoroughly searched	(C)

M. Chun
Col Comdg 27th Infty Brigade RFA

Comdg 27th Infty Brigade RFA

Vol 6

Confidential

West Germany
(2-91 Bu RM
from 29/5/77 to 3/6/77

Coy

Army Form C. 2118.

WAR DIARY "Y" Bde RHA
or
INTELLIGENCE SUMMARY.
(Erase heading not required.)

Instructions regarding War Diaries and Intelligence Summaries are contained in F. S. Regs., Part II. and the Staff Manual respectively. Title pages will be prepared in manuscript.

Place	Date	Hour	Summary of Events and Information	Remarks and references to Appendices
Battle Hd. Qrs 1,2,3,6			~~strikethrough~~	
			~~strikethrough~~	
Do	23/4/17	10am	The Sgt. Maj. Brig. R.H.A. who had formed part of 7th Div. Arty. Group was taken over by 58th Divisional Arty.	
Do	24/4/17	1pm	The Sgt. Maj. Brig. R.H.A. were taken over by 7th Div. Arty.	
Do	25/4/17		The relief of the Brigade by 35th Div. Artillery commenced	
Do	30/4/17	10am	The relief of the Brigade completed. The Brigade was withdrawn from action and went into rest.	
			Casualties during the month of April 13 O.R. wounded. 1 O.R. shock from	
			shell.	
			M. Peters	
			Lt. Col.	
			a/c Y Bde RHA	
			Country Sgt for Example RHA	

WAR DIARY
or
INTELLIGENCE SUMMARY.
(Erase heading not required.)

Army Form C. 2118.

291st Brigade R.H.A.

Place	Date	Hour	Summary of Events and Information	Remarks and references to Appendices
ERVILLERS	7/7/17	4.45 am	The Brigade marched to FRICOURT camping in MAMETZ BRIGADE CAMP	(22)
FRICOURT	11/7/17	6 am	The Brigade marched to YTRES camping on the Southern end of VALLULART WOOD	(20)
YTRES	12/7/17		Section of each Battery relieved sections of 291st Brigade covering the front of 173rd Infantry Brigade	(22)
Do	18/7/17		The relief of the 290th Brigade R.H.A. completed by 291st Brigade. Battle Head Quarters being south of METZ-en-COUTURE at Q.27.c.4.4. The Brigade formed the Right Group of 58th Divisional Front.	(22)
METZ en COUTURE	29/7/17	12.45 am	Raid carried out by a detachment from the 4th Royal Fusilier Londn Regt. the raid was successful but found no Bosche in PLUSH TRENCH. In addition to fire from of 291st Brig. R.H.A., 6-18 pm, 4-45 stors of 290th and 5-18 pm of 181st Brigade R.F.A. were placed on the disposal of O/C commanding Right Group.	(20) (22)

N. Olam
Comdg R.H.A.
291st Brig R.H.A.

WAR DIARY
or
INTELLIGENCE SUMMARY
291st Brigade R.F.A.

(Erase heading not required.)

Place	Date 1917	Hour	Summary of Events and Information	Remarks and references to Appendices
HARINCOURT	1/8	10 a.m.	The Brigade formed part of 9th Division 4th Corps 3rd Army	
-do-	3/8	10 a.m.	" " " " of 40th Division 3rd Corps 3rd Army	
-do-	2/8	8 a.m.	Half Brigade moved to take over from 51st Brigade R.F.A. at Boyelle	
Boyelle	5/8	8 a.m.	2nd Half of Brigade moved to Boyelle and relief completed at 12 noon. The Brigade coming under orders of 2nd Divl Artillery 7th Corps 3rd Army	
ST LEGER	6/8	10 p.m.	D.C.D. Battery moved 1 gun each into new position near ST LEGER VALLEY	
"	7/8	12 noon	The Brigade formed part of 3rd Divisional Artillery but in VI Corps 3rd Army	
ST LEGER	8/8	12 noon	Head Quarters moved to ST LEGER and B.C. & D. Batteries moved the remainder of their guns	
ST LEGER & ERVILLERS	20/8 21/8	11.30 p.m. 3 p.m.	Guns into new positions. Batteries went into action from new positions to support two attacks at ERVILLERS Advance party went to WINNEZEELE in Flanders	
"	26/8	8.30 p.m.	Head Quarters marched to ARRAS & entrained for the north.	
HONDPOUTRE	27/8	2.30 p.m.	Arrived at HONDPOUTRE and advanced & composite at this place	
DICKEBUSCHE	30/8 31/8	7 p.m.	Brigade moved into new Wagon Lines in this area	
"	31/8		Half Batteries (personnel) moved into the lines near YPRES and took over from 10th Australian Divisional Artillery.	

M. ?
Lt. Col.
Comdg 291st Brigade R.F.A.

WAR DIARY or INTELLIGENCE SUMMARY

Army Form C. 2118.

235th Brigade R.F.A.

Vol 9

Place	Date	Hour	Summary of Events and Information	Remarks and references to Appendices
Brickstacks	2/9		Half Battaries withdrew from position south of Ypres.	
	3/9	7.30 am	Marched to billets WEST of HERZEELE. At noon men transferred from II Corps to XVIII Corps.	
HERZEELE	6/9	8.20	Brigade Staff and one section per Battery, proceeded to his wagon lines. B.C. & 1 section per Battery went into action and took over from LEFT GROUP R.D.A.	
"	7/9	8.20	Remainder of Batteries arrived and went into action.	
VLAMATINGE			Lt. Col. C. Clifford Angus took over mr. command of 1 SG? from 2 Major at La Belle	
	14/9	12 noon	Lt. Col. W.T.O.Dam Cmdg Sg. 284th Bg. took over mr. command.	
La Belle Alliance	20/9	5.40 am	Supported the attack of 174th Brigade on the St. JULIAN front. Attack completely successful. Received letter from Brig. Gen. Hyssop O.C. Commdg 174th Brigade congratulating the group on its fine Gunnery.	
	26/9	5.50 am	Supported an attack by 175th Brigade which was successful. 2nd Lt. O'Brien Killed	
	30/9	12 noon	Lt. Col. C. Clifford assumed command of the support.	

M. Ryan
Lt. Col.
Cmdg 235th Brigade R.F.A.

C. Clifford
Lt. Col.
Cmdg 235th Brigade R.F.A.

WAR DIARY
OR
INTELLIGENCE SUMMARY.
(Erase heading not required.)

Army Form C. 2118.

291st Brigade R.F.A.

Place	Date	Hour	Summary of Events and Information	Remarks and references to Appendices
In the Field	5/10/17	—	Covered the Infantry of 48th Divn in action	(M¹)
— do —	10/10/17	—	Covered the Infantry of 48th Divn in action	(M²)
— do —	16/10/17	—	Covered the Infantry of 48th Divn in action	(M³)
— do —	22/10/17	—	Covered the Infantry of 63rd (R.N.) Divn in action	(M⁴)
— do —	29/10/17	—	Covered the Infantry of 63rd (R.N.) Divn in action	(M⁵)
			Casualties period in action 5/10/17 to 30/10/17	(M⁶)
			Officers — Killed 2, wounded 1, gassed 8 shock 1 — Total 21	
			O.R. — Killed 23 died of wounds 13, wounded 138 gassed 36, sick 75 — Total 285	(M⁷)
			Immediate awards for above period —	(M⁸)
			Officers — DSO 1, MC 3	(M⁹)
			O.R. — DCM 3, MM 14	(M¹⁰)

Lieut-Colonel, R.F.A. (T.)
Commanding 291st (London) Brigade R.F.A. (T.)

WAR DIARY
INTELLIGENCE SUMMARY

Place	Date	Hour	Summary of Events and Information	Remarks and references to Appendices
HQ Wormhoudt	Oct 31/19	—	2 Sections of Batteries in action were relieved by sections of 39th Bde. R.F.A.	
do	Nov 1/19	—	Relief completed.	
do	Nov 2/19	—	Brigade marched to WORMHOUDT area	
Wormhoudt	Nov 3/19	—	Brigade marched to RECQUES area	
NURLU NIEURLET	Nov 12/19	—	Brigade marched to ESTREHE area	

Immediate awards for above period:—
Officers — Nil.
O.R. — Nil.

WAR DIARY
or
INTELLIGENCE SUMMARY.
(Erase heading not required.)

291st Brigade R.F.A.

Army Form C. 2118.

Place	Date	Hour	Summary of Events and Information	Remarks and references to Appendices
BHQ Okom	Dec 4.1917		Brigade proceded by road via THIEMBRONNE, NIEURLET and WORMHOUDT to Wagon lines EVERDINGHE arriving 8/12/17.	
Elverdinghe	Dec 9.1917		Sections of Batteries relieved Sections of Batteries of 250th Brigade, RFA in the line covering the Infantry of 58th Division.	
Capple House	Dec 10.12.1917		Relief of 250th Brigade, RFA, by 291st Brigade, RFA Completed. Lieut-Colonel J.F. Halland, CMG, DSO, RFA assumed temporary Command of Brigade.	
" "	9.12.1917		Lieut-Colonel N.S. Odam, RFA (T) resumed Command of Brigade.	
" "	31.12.1917			

Casualties during period 1st to 31st December, 1917.

Officers - Nil
Other Ranks - Killed 6, wounded 6.

C.M.Lain
Lieut.-Colonel, R.F.A. (T.)
Commanding 291st (London) Brigade R.F.A. (T.)

Army Form C. 2118.

WAR DIARY
or
INTELLIGENCE SUMMARY. 291st Brigade, R.F.A.
(Erase heading not required.)

Instructions regarding War Diaries and Intelligence Summaries are contained in F. S. Regs., Part II. and the Staff Manual respectively. Title pages will be prepared in manuscript.

Place	Date	Hour	Summary of Events and Information	Remarks and references to Appendices
B.H.Q.	1-11/4/18		Scheme of Battery relief by 159th Army Brigade R.F.A.	A.R. 22/1 A.R.
Oneux	13/4/18		Relief completed	A.R.
Plandrugh	27/28/4/18		Brigade proceeded by rail to MIERS BRETONNEUX for relief at DOMART - SOMME	A.R. A.R. A.R. A.R.
Domart	28/4/18		Brigade marched by road to CARREPUIS	A.R.
Carrepuis	29/4/18		Brigade marched by road to BRETIGNY	A.R.
Bretigny	30/4/18		Relief of French Artillery in the line commenced.	A.R.
	31/4/18		Relief in progress	A.R.

[signature]

WAR DIARY or **INTELLIGENCE SUMMARY**
(Erase heading not required.)

Army Form C. 2118.

291st Brigade R.F.A.

Place	Date	Hour	Summary of Events and Information	Remarks and references to Appendices
RFO Villete	1/7/18		Relief of French Artillery in the line completed, covering Infty of 30th Divn.	
do	31/7/18		181st HQ moved to SINCENY. Wagon Lines moved from BRETIGNY to VILETTE.	
Sinceny	15/7/18		Covered the Infantry of 58th Divn in the line	
do	22/7/18		Covered the Infantry of 58th Divn in the line	
do	28/7/18		Covered the Infantry of 58th Divn in the line	
Blerancourt	18/1/18		Command of Brigade assumed by Lieut Col AMW Dudley vice H Col M Odam. ANW Dudley July 1918 – 10th October	

Hurl Smith
Major
Lieut. Colonel, R.F.A.
Commanding 291st (London) Brigade R.F.A. (T.)

Casualties during July 1918 – 10th October

WAR DIARY
or
INTELLIGENCE SUMMARY.

Army Form C. 2118.

291st Brigade, R.F.A.

Place	Date	Hour	Summary of Events and Information	Remarks and references to Appendices
B.H.Q.	March 1918			
	1st		Covered the Infantry of 58th Division in the line	a/r
-do-	19th		407th and 408th Batteries of 96th Army Brigade R.F.A. attached to 291st Bde R.F.A.	a/r
-do-	21st		Enemy offensive commenced. B.H.Q. withdrawn to PIERREMANDE	a/r
Cinvmands	31st		Covered the Infantry of 58th Division in the line.	a/r
			Casualties during period 1st to 31st March 1918.	a/r
			Officers (407th Bty) 1 wounded	a/r
			Other Ranks — 2 killed 7 wounded (2-407 Bty)	a/r

A. Dutsy
Lieut.-Colonel, R.F.A.
Commanding 291st (London) Brigade R.F.A. (T.)

58th Div.

WAR DIARY

Headquarters,

291st BRIGADE, R.F.A.

A P R I L

1 9 1 8

Army Form C. 2118.

WAR DIARY
or
INTELLIGENCE SUMMARY. 291st Brigade, R.F.A.   Vol 16
(Erase heading not required.)

Instructions regarding War Diaries and Intelligence Summaries are contained in F. S. Regs., Part II. and the Staff Manual respectively. Title pages will be prepared in manuscript.

Place	Date	Hour	Summary of Events and Information	Remarks and references to Appendices
BHQ Fernemoude	April 1/1918		6 Batteries in action in Sneering Authoille area covering Boyssen front. Chaney Bridges & Condren, also Bosken front Amigny Rony and Servais	AR
			Brigade relieved by French Artillery Regiment on the line	AR
-do-	2nd		Brigade marched to Longpont and provided by train from there to Longpont	AR
	14/5		4 Batteries in action night 6th/7th guns each covering Villers Bretonneux front	AR
Bois d'Aill	6th		to Vaire Wood. Remaining sections to R.A.Detail, 58th Div on 7th inst	AR
Londilley	7/23rd		Battery positions O.Ps consolidated. Infantry consolidated. Counter preparation carried out at night. Shoots of tri on places of assembly, roads, tracks &c	AR
	24th		Enemy attack opened at 5:15 am. Infantry relays and Batteries withdrawn to cover Villers Bretonneux flanks. 8pm 24th Batteries moved forward to support a successful attack launched at 10pm same day	AR
	25/29th		Infantry consolidated and continued concentrations carried out	AR
	28/29th 29/30th		Brigade relieved in the line by 86th Army Brigade R.F.A.	AR
	30th		Brigade marched to ST PIERRE about — en route to LONG area to refit.	AR

A. Dudley
Lieut.-Colonel, R.F.A.
Commanding, 291st (London) Brigade R.F.A. (T.)

Army Form C. 2118.

WAR DIARY
INTELLIGENCE SUMMARY.
(Erase heading not required.)

Place	Date	Hour	Summary of Events and Information	Remarks and references to Appendices
Burgy &c.Abb.	May 3rd 1918		Brigade marched by road to PONT REMY area	a.a
Pont Remy	16th		Brigade marched by road to BOURDON	a.a
Bourdon	17th		Brigade proceeded to CONTAY and Sections relieved sections of 282nd Brigade RFA in the line	a.a
Visa b 3	18th		Relief completed. D Battery RFA attached to 291st Brigade, R.F.A. forming left Group. 58th Divisional Artillery and covering Infantry of 35th Division in the line.	a.a a.a a.a
do	16/30a		Routes of fire on roads. Wireless communication to Count. Preparations and Nightfiring programmes carried out from Positions O.P's constructed and improved.	a.a a.a
do	31st		As usual 35th Division on left in operations for AVELUY WOOD Bombardment carried out by Group.	a.a

A.V. Kirby
Lieut.-Colonel, R.F.A.
Commanding 291st (London) Brigade R.F.A. (T.)

WAR DIARY "229½ Brigade, R.A."

Army Form C. 2118.

INTELLIGENCE SUMMARY.
(Erase heading not required.)

Instructions regarding War Diaries and Intelligence Summaries are contained in F.S. Regs., Part II. and the Staff Manual respectively. Title pages will be prepared in manuscript.

Place	Date	Hour	Summary of Events and Information	Remarks and references to Appendices
HQ Sy Bois	June 1918			
Sus Sy B3	1st		Covering the Infantry of 18th Division in the line	A/D
	7th		Brigade relieved by 168th Army Brigade RFA in the line	A/D
Contay	9th		Brigade marched by road to ST SAUVEUR, forming part of 22nd Corps R.A. Reserve	A/D
				A/D
St Sauveur	11th		B.C.s having and St French Corps Area reconnoitred by BC's	
to	19th		Brigade marched by road to BACKINCOURT area	20/20
Bavincourt	20th		Relieved 235th Brigade RFA 47th DA in the line, forming Right	20/20
			Group. 58th DA with 474 Hay By tB and B/108 Army Bde RFA attached	20/20
D.7.a.8.7.	21st		Harassing fire carried out by day & night on roads, trenches,	A/D
Sheet 51 D	30		tracks and bridges; also MG emplacements & Mine etc	20/20
	30		Assisted 16th Division on left in bombardment of enemy trench systems	A/D

Lieut.-Colonel, R.F.A.
Commanding 229th (London) Brigade R.F.A. (T.F.)

WAR DIARY or **INTELLIGENCE SUMMARY**

Army Form C. 2118.

291 Brigade, R.F.A.

(Erase heading not required.)

Place	Date	Hour	Summary of Events and Information	Remarks and references to Appendices
D1a81 Sheet 62D	July 12. 1916		Operated 58" Australian Batn on right in raiding enemy trenches by 4 Batteries	JCJ
	13"		A/C Bty 105" Army Brigade, R.F.A attached Right Group	JCJ
	14"		A/B Bty 108" Army Brigade, R.F.A withdrew to Nagymers	JCJ
	21"		Co-operated in gas bombardment of enemy trenches and back to	JCJ
	25"		Assisted in raid on enemy trenches, co-operating with Australian Group, 7 Batteries in action, Zero 10am.	JCJ
	28"		Two Chinese attacks, put down acc. to standing orders by 5th Aust Division Group, Constituting left Group with	JCJ
	29"		A/C/86 Bde R.F.A formed Group, Constituting left Group with 290" Bde R.F.A as Sub-Group	JCJ

JC Janning? Capt.
fr Major, R.F.A.
Comdg 291 Brigade, R.F.A.

58th Divl. Artillery

291st BRIGADE, R. F. A.

AUGUST, 1918

WAR DIARY
INTELLIGENCE SUMMARY.
(Erase heading not required.)

291st BRIGADE R.F.A.

Aug 6 Nov

Army Form C. 2118.

Place	Date	Hour	Summary of Events and Information	Remarks and references to Appendices
B.H.Q.	Aug			
Rose Post Lab's Grand Bailin				
3rd 622 RE 62c MH				
1/30 oct Corbie	2nd		Brigade relieved by 112th Brigade, 25th Division R.F.A. in the line. Batteries bivouac fires at Bavincourt.	AX
Henencourt	8th		Open in attack with 9th Group near 58th D.A.	AX
	9th		Batteries advanced positions near Sailly-Laurette.	AX
Tailles Knoll	10th		Attack continued under 4th Australian D.A. & Batteries advanced positions	AX
Morcourt			1800	
Pear	11/12th		Advance made by Canadian Wood continuing & Western Valley & southern of	AX
Western Valley			division force.	
Bouzencourt	13/15th		Batteries & Bray, arrived by 3rd Australian D.A. Batteries advanced	AX
			position east of Bray Division	
Bouzent Valley	26th		Brigade moved forward to position gone of Bray, under 58th D.A.	AX
	27th		Attack continued. Batteries advanced positions in Bouzent Valley	AX
Mesnilly day	28th		Batteries advanced Chipille to Buire. A further advance was made	AX
Buire			and positions taken up near the Bellows of Mem	RX
Mon	31st		Batteries advanced positions at Junction of Roeux Valley & Hill 110	AX
100 B/10			and attack continued	

R. Smyth Lt Col RFA
Comdg 291 Bde RFA

WAR DIARY or INTELLIGENCE SUMMARY

Army Form C.2118.

291 Brigade R.F.A.   Vol 21

Place	Date	Hour	Summary of Events and Information	Remarks and references to Appendices
Withybrook H8 ARHEM	Sept 1/18	11/30 pm	Batteries moved to HAUT ALLAINES attack continued	
"	"	6ᵃ	Batteries moved to E. of AIZECOURT-LE-HAUT.	
"	"	"	Brigade withdrawn and moved N. of AIZECOURT-LE-HAUT under 58 Div Arty only covering Infantry of 58 Div.	
AIZECOURT-LE-BAS	"	7ᵃ	Infantry 58 Div attacked. Brigade withdrawn into reserve at AIZECOURT-LE-BAS	
AIZECOURT-LE-BAS	"	9ᵃ	In action near GRYENCOURT, covering attack by 58 Div on PEZIERES and EPEHY	
QUARRY E158	"	10ᵃ	Withdrawn into reserve at AIZECOURT-LE-BAS	
"	"	17ᵃ	Moved into action near VILLERS-FAUCON under 18th Div only.	
"	"	18ᵃ	Attack on EPEHY, PEZIERES and RONSSOY and LEMPIRE, Batteries advanced 16E3 ord.	
"	"	19ᵃ	Attack continued by 53rd Infantry Brigade, 18th Division.	
"	"	21ᵃ	Attack continued for ground 2. of RONSSOY	
"	"	24ᵃ	Enemy counter attack smashed by concentrates Arty fire on TOMBOIS VALLEY F3d	
Mt RONSSOY	"	25ᵃ	Covering Infantry of 27th American Div under H.Q. Div Arty.	
"	"	27ᵃ	Gas bombardment of hostile battery positions with "BB" shell	
"	"	29ᵃ	Commenced attack on HINDENBURG LINE at LE CATELET and covt. by 27th Amer Div.	

R Kingdom
Lieut. Colonel, R.F.A.
Commanding 291st (London) Brigade R.F.A. (T.F.)

58 DT

WAR DIARY
INTELLIGENCE SUMMARY

Army Form C. 2118.

of 291 Brigade, RFA

Place	Date	Hour	Summary of Events and Information	Remarks and references to Appendices
MAP 9 Nr BELLICOURT	1918 Oct 9	1ᵖ	Attacks for LE CATELET provided - Batteries covering Infantry of 27ᵗʰ Amer. Divn.	
LE CATELET		4ᵖ	Batteries advanced to position in GOUY covering Infantry of 38ᵗʰ Divn.	
—do—		8ᵖ	Attack for VILLERS-OUTREAUX commenced by 38ᵗʰ Divn.	
—do—		9ᵖ	Brigade withdrew to Wagon lines in LONGAVESNES area.	
AIZECOURT-LE-BAS		11ᵗʰ	Entrained at PÉRONNE.	
MAROC		12ᵗʰ	Detrained at BULLY-GRENAY to billets at MAROC.	
DOURGES		15ᵗʰ	Brigade marched to DOURGES en route to line.	
AUCHY		19ᵗʰ	Relieved 146ᵗʰ Army Bde RFA, C/291 Battery in action near ORCHIES.	
AIX		20ᵗʰ	Brigade advanced from near ORCHIES to AIX - C/291 advanced in action near ORCHIES. Remainder of Brigade in main Guard - Covering 175ᵗʰ Infy Bde, 58ᵗʰ Divn.	
—do—		21	Advance continued to RONGY.	
—do—		22	Registration having and mine cutting vicinity of FORTE DE MAULDE.	
—do—		26	C/D Batteries advanced to RUE DOMBRÉ, after Enemy in a evacuating F?E DE MAULDE	
—do—		27	Relieved by 290ᵗʰ Brigade, R.F.A. Withdrew to AIX in Divisional Reserve.	
—do—		31	In Divisional reserve.	

R Kemp Well
Lieut. Colonel, R.F.A.
Commanding 291st (London) Brigade R.F.A. (T.)

WAR DIARY
INTELLIGENCE SUMMARY.
(Erase heading not required.)

291 Brigade, R.F.A.

Army Form C. 2118.

Place	Date	Hour	Summary of Events and Information	Remarks and references to Appendices
AIX	1918 Nov 1st		In Divisional Reserve	
	6th	8ᵃ	Brigade marched to MIERS, sections of "B" and "D" Batteries covering advance of 175th Infantry Brigade	
MIERS	9th		Advance continued to ECACHERIES. Sections of "B" and "D" Btys in action	
ECACHERIES	11th		Hostilities ceased at 1100 hours	
	21st		Brigade marched to billets in MIERS area	
MIERS	29th		Brigade marched to billets in BELOEIL area	

N Campbell Lieut Colonel, R.F.A.
Comdg 291 Brigade, R.F.A.

Army Form C. 2118.

WAR DIARY
INTELLIGENCE SUMMARY.
(Erase heading not required.)

29. Brigade. R.F.A.

Place	Date	Hour	Summary of Events and Information	Remarks and references to Appendices
BELOEIL- BELGIUM	1918 Dec 1st to Dec 30th		Recreational & Educational training carried out. Courses, Schools and Demobilization released for demobilization.	N:L

A. Kemp Welch Lt Col.

Army Form C. 2118.

WAR DIARY
~~INTELLIGENCE SUMMARY~~
(Erase heading not required.)

291ST LONDON BRIGADE, R.F.A.

Instructions regarding War Diaries and Intelligence Summaries are contained in F. S. Regs., Part II. and the Staff Manual respectively. Title pages will be prepared in manuscript.

Place	Date	Hour	Summary of Events and Information	Remarks and references to Appendices
B.H.Q. BEROEIL. BELGIUM.	April 1919 1st to 30th		Nil	

Lieut Col. H.M.H.
br Major, R.J.A.
Commanding 291. Brigade, R.J.A.

WAR DIARY
INTELLIGENCE SUMMARY.
(Erase heading not required.)

Army Form C. 2118.

Place	Date	Hour	Summary of Events and Information	Remarks and references to Appendices
B.H.Q. BEKOEIL BELGIUM.	MAY 1st to 31st		Nil	

Arnould Capt Adjt.

M PRIOR
Lieut Colonel, B.F.A.
Commanding 235th (London) Brigade R.F.A.

WO 95/2995/5

58TH DIVISION

TRENCH MORTAR BATTYS.
MAR 1917-DEC 1918

Box 2995

Trench Mortar Batterys

WAR DIARY
of
INTELLIGENCE SUMMARY.
(Erase heading not required.)

Army Form C. 2118.

Vol 1

Place	Date	Hour	Summary of Events and Information	Remarks and references to Appendices
	March 1917 1st		All Batteries left III Army T.M. School.	ord
Lallin	2nd		V/58, X/58, & Y/58, less one section, 7th Batteries moved to GROSVILLE. X/58 and one section of Y/58 Battery moved to BERLES-AU-BOIS.	ord
	3rd		Taking over stores and equipment from 49th Divisional T.M. Batteries.	ord
	4th		Took over from 49th Division on the Line. Carried out schemes between 5.0 & 9.0 p.m. 21 rounds fired on the OSIERBED and enemy trenches in front of RANSART by V/58 & Z/58 7th Batteries. 14 rounds fired by V/58 7th B. on the TALUS and the BLOCKHOUSE. Rourke's dugouts.	ord
	5th		6 rounds fired at enemy strong point by V/58 Battery. Rourke's dugouts. Every available man from trench Batteries employed in improving emplacements and clearing ammunition, both of which were handed over in a very neglected state.	ord
	6th		Work continued on emplacements and ammunition.	ord
	7th		Work continued on emplacements and ammunition.	ord
	8th		4 rounds fired by V/58 7th Battery at enemy strong point. 4 rounds fired by V/58 Battery at Sap Z.9 at request of Infantry. Results of both shoots satisfactory. Sap Z.9.A. destroyed. Autumn Batteries continued work on emplacements and ammunition.	

WAR DIARY
or
INTELLIGENCE SUMMARY.
(Erase heading not required.)

Army Form C. 2118.

Instructions regarding War Diaries and Intelligence Summaries are contained in F. S. Regs., Part II. and the Staff Manual respectively. Title pages will be prepared in manuscript.

Place	Date	Hour	Summary of Events and Information	Remarks and references to Appendices
Zulu		6"	16 rounds fired by Y/55 TM Battery on Tap M.Z.9.a. as assistance to Y/58 Battery. Results satisfactory.	wind
		9"	20 rounds fired by Z/58 Battery at enemy wire opposite CAVENDISH Sap. Results satisfactory. Enemy inhibition caused of in first 7 rounds. 5 rounds retaliation fired by X/58 Battery at enemy front line north of MONCHY. Results satisfactory. 16 rounds fired by Y/58 Battery in support of patrol sent out to examine Sap. Z.9.a. Results satisfactory. Work continued on emplacement and ammunition.	wind
		10"	42 rounds fired by Z/58 TM Battery at enemy wire opposite CAVENDISH Sap. A large number of duds and faulty to fairly line and fairly twin striker cap. It was found that the number of duds could be reduced by tying on striker cap before firing. 90 rounds fired by Y/58 TM Battery at enemy wire north of FICHEUX. Results satisfactory and lanes cut 20 yards wide. Emplacements and beds in letter order in this sector and consequently results of shooting more satisfactory. Y/58 TM Battery registered on the BLOCKHOUSE with satisfactory results.	wind
		11"	48 rounds fired by Z/58 TM Battery at wire opposite CAVENDISH Sap. Results more satisfactory as the new striker caps were tried on. 61 rounds fire by Y/58 Battery	wind

WAR DIARY
of
INTELLIGENCE SUMMARY.
(Erase heading not required.)

Army Form C. 2118.

Place	Date	Hour	Summary of Events and Information	Remarks and references to Appendices
Field	11 cont.		at enemy wire north of FICHEUX and on the RANSART salient. Results very satisfactory north of FICHEUX but Lines satisfactory owing to faulty wire, opposite RANSART salient. 30 rounds fired by X/58 T.M. Battery at enemy wire north of MONCHY salient. Result satisfactory. Gun cut about 8 yards wide. R.E. squad and fatigue party worked during night on the M.G. gun emplacements opposite RANSART salient. Other emplacements also improved.	W.D.
	12th		46 rounds fired by Z/58 T.M. Battery at enemy wire opposite CAVENDISH Sap. Results satisfactory. Gun nearly 30 yards wide cut. 16 rounds fired by Y/58 Battery at enemy wire north of FICHEUX. Gun 20 yards wide maintained. 35 rounds fired by X/58 Battery at enemy wire north of MONCHY. Gun cut about 8 yards wide. Enemy had repaired this wire during previous night. 10 rounds fired by Y/58 Battery at wire opposite RANSART. Both emplacements badly damaged by enemy shell fire and by chaps. R.E. party again worked during night to repair these emplacements. V/58 Th Battery registered on LES TROIS MAISONS. Results satisfactory. Great difficulty experienced in supplying Heavy Ammunition to the emplacements owing to the condition of the ground and the thaw.	W.D.
	13th		29 rounds fired by Z/58 T.M. Battery at wire opposite CAVENDISH Sap. Result very satisfactory	

Army Form C. 2118.

WAR DIARY
or
INTELLIGENCE SUMMARY.
(Erase heading not required.)

Place	Date	Hour	Summary of Events and Information	Remarks and references to Appendices
Field	13th Cont.		Lane 40 yards wide cut. 65 rounds fired by Y/58 Battery at enemy wire north of FICHEUX. Lane 50 yards wide cut. 45 rounds fired by X/58 Battery at wire north of MONCHY. Lane about 20 yards wide. 30 rounds fired by Y/58 Battery at wire opposite RANSART.	wnd
	14th		40 rounds fired by Y/58 Battery at enemy wire opposite RANSART. Lane cut 20 yards wide. Gun pits cut of action by enemy shelling and pits destroyed. The good whereupon of Gunners Finch & Davis reported both G.R.D. 40 rounds fired by X/58 7th Battery at wire north of MONCHY, lane cut 20 yards wide. 50 rounds fired by Y/58 Battery at wire north of FICHEUX lane maintained 40 yards wide. 30 yards fired by Z/58 Battery at wire opposite CAVENDISH Sap, lane maintained 40 yards wide. 14 rounds fired in	wnd
	x 15th		retaliation by Y/58 Battery. Results observed satisfactory. x 160 rounds fired by the hudson Battery to improve gaps in wire. Result satisfactory. 14 rounds fired by V/58 Battery in retaliation.	wnd
	16th		hudson enfilments repaired. 3 rounds fired in registration by Y/58 Battery	wnd
	17th		124 rounds fired by hudson Battery to improve gaps. Result satisfactory.	wnd
	18th		Enemy evacuated his trenches	wnd
	19th		hudson arm outhod and crew trails at GROSVILLE and BERLES.	wnd
	20th		Ammunition collected, trailers cleaned. Two trench mortars sent to I.O.M.	wnd

Army Form C. 2118.

WAR DIARY
INTELLIGENCE SUMMARY.
(Erase heading not required.)

Instructions regarding War Diaries and Intelligence Summaries are contained in F. S. Regs., Part II. and the Staff Manual respectively. Title pages will be prepared in manuscript.

Place	Date	Hour	Summary of Events and Information	Remarks and references to Appendices
Field	21st		Personal concentration at BERLES	W.D.
	22		Fatigue party 25 men to assist D.A.C.	W.D.
	23		Fatigue party 50 men to assist D.A.C. at Achiet. Personal move to GAUDIEMPRE	W.D.
	24		Stores, equipment, Medium Batteries concentration at GAUDIEMPRE	W.D.
	25		D.A.C. began collecting ammunition left in F. Sector.	W.D.

W. Smyth
C.W.D. Lt.Col.
25/3/17.

Vol 3

CONFIDENTIAL
****

WAR DIARY

OF

58ᵗʰ B.A.C.A.B.

From 1/1/5/17
To 31/5/17

WAR DIARY of 58th D.I. Trench Mortar Batteries

INTELLIGENCE SUMMARY.
(Erase heading not required.)

Army Form C. 2118.

Place	Date	Hour	Summary of Events and Information	Remarks and references to Appendices
Field	1917 16 May		Two 2" Trench Mortars taken over from 7' Division in BULLECOURT Sector reference ECOUST-ST-MEIN Edition 3 1:10000 M 28 a 2.2. by 1st detachment X/58th T.M.By	
	18"	10am	X Battery detachment relieved in line by 2nd detachment of X Battery	
	19"		06 V/58 T.M. B'ty proceeded to V Army T.M. School taking one 2" Trench Mortars of Y/58" B'ty with him	
	W		½ Debenborg of 12 men from V B'ty reported to CRUCIFIX CORNER dump	
			½ to Debenborg for duty	
	20"	6am	X B'ty detachment relieved in line by 3rd detachment of X B'ty	
		9am	2 medium T Mortars ready for action in new position at U 27 c 7.8.	
	22"	10am	X B'ty detachment relieved in line by 1st detachment of Z B'ty	
	24"	"	" " " " " 2nd "	
	25"	mid- night	Z " " " " " 3rd "	
	26"		Instruction in trier grenades by instructors attached to 58th D.A.C.	
	27"	mid- night	Z B'ty detachment relieved in line by 1st detachment of Z B'ty	
	29"		Z " " " " " " " X B'ty	
	31st	2am	X B'ty detachment withdrawn from line. Shown	

31-5-1917.

O.B.Warner
O/Ch. 58th Lieutant R.F.A.
O/Ch. 58th D.I.T.M.B.

Army Form C. 2118.

WAR DIARY
INTELLIGENCE SUMMARY.
(Erase heading not required.)

Instructions regarding War Diaries and Intelligence Summaries are contained in F.S. Regs., Part II. and the Staff Manual respectively. Title pages will be prepared in manuscript.

Vol I

Place	Date	Hour	Summary of Events and Information	Remarks and references to Appendices
Field	19.17	Vichy	Two 2" Trench Mortars taken over from 7th Division in BULLECOURT. Reference ECOUST-st-MEIN Edition 3 1/10,000, U 28 a 2.2. by 1st detachment X/51st M. Bty	
	18th	6am	X Battery detachment relieved in lines by 2nd detachment of X Battery	
	19		O.C. Y/51 T.M. B'ty proceeded to V Army T.M. School taking one 2" Trench Mortar of Y/51 B'ty with him.	
	20		1st Detachment of 12 men from V B'ty reported to CRUCIFIX CORNER about BEHAGNIES for duty.	
	20th	6am	X B'ty detachment relieved in lines by 3rd detachment of X B'ty	
		9am	2 medium Mortars ready for action in new position at U.27 c 9.8.	
	22	6am	X B'ty detachment relieved in line by 1st detachment of Z B'ty	
	24		Z " " " 2nd " "	
	25	mid night	Z " " " 3rd " "	
	26	–	Instruction in Anti-gas methods by Instructors attached to 55th D.A.C.	
	27 mid night	Z B'ty detachment relieved in line by 1st detachment of Z B'ty	
	29		Z " " " 1st " " of X B'ty	
	31st	2am	X B'ty detachment withdrawn from lines - thence	

31st May 1917

A.R.M...
Major R.F.A.
O.C. T.M.O. 51st D.A.

Army Form C. 2118.

WAR DIARY of 58th Div Hty French Mortar Batteries
INTELLIGENCE SUMMARY. for June 1917.
(Erase heading not required.)

V.M.II

Place	Date	Hour	Summary of Events and Information	Remarks and references to Appendices
Field	1st	-	Camps moved from to (Sheet 57c 20,000) B 28 a 8.8.	
	2nd	-	Lieut Hooke & 1 N.C.O. sent to Headquarters of Corps Heavy Artillery at ACHIET-LE-GRAND for collection of ammunition in backward areas. D.T.M.O. & X/58th T.M.By proceeded to BULLECOURT to centralise 2" mortars and ammunition. 2 - 2" mortars & 25 rounds of ammn at U 27c 8.8. ECOUST ST MEIN 1/10,000	
	3rd		1 N.C.O. & 20 men detailed for work at Divisional Bombing dump MORY.	
	4th		10 Officers & N.C.O.s sent to 290' Brigade for work as pioneers - 3 telephonists and 10 Ammunition numbers - 3 Officers & 24 other ranks proceeded on course to 5th Army Trench Mortar School VALHEUREUX.	
	5th		2 Officers & 11 other ranks sent out collecting shell cases. 12 French 3 grenn to MORY dump.	
	6th		Capt Tillery, O.C. V/58th T.M. By, selected position for 1 Heavy Mortar at BULLECOURT U 26 c 7.6. 100 rds. T 9.45 ammn brought to Mory lines	
	7th		100 rds mortar taken up to Gun position of V.B.Ty, Gun put into commission. Lieut Gudgeon & 2nd Lt Hamlett to BULLECOURT to select position for 2" Mortars.	
	8th		Capt Tillery O.C. V.B.Ty killed by shell & 2 men buried by debris. Position in MORY cemetery. Capt Tillery carried (Asst funeral)	
	9th		2 men of V.B.Ty. killed, 2 men wounded. Lieut Gudgeon took over V.B.Ty. Asst Bolton of Y.B.Ty went into action at BULLECOURT.	
	10th		New position for V.B.Ty selected by Lieut Gudgeon at U 21 c 2.3.	
	11		Y.B.Ty fired 5 rounds from 2" Mortars position (ranging).	
	12		Y.B.Ty fired 19 rounds. 2nd Lieut Elden posted to V/58th T.M.By temporarily.	

Army Form C. 2118.

WAR DIARY
or
INTELLIGENCE SUMMARY.
(Erase heading not required.)

June 1917

Place	Date	Hour	Summary of Events and Information	Remarks and references to Appendices
Field	13	5am	Y/58 relieved in line by Y/58 & 116 Bty. 40 rounds fired by Z Bty.	
	14		V/58 Guns ready to fire. Gun pit & dug-out completed.	
	16		20 rounds fired by Z Bty, last shot premature, but required remaking.	
	17	5am	2" Mortar turned in by enemy shell fire dug out blown in, no casualties. 2nd detachment of Z/58 relieved by 1st detachment.	
	19		Y/58 & C Battn. relieved by 58 DA & Y Bty. Y/58 & C Battn. proceeded to VALHEUREUX on course of 2" Mortar Newspaper in BULLECOURT for 2" Mortars in course of preparation	
	23rd	10am	4 Heavy Trench Mortars & 2 mes complete (in line) handed over to the DTMO 7" Division	
	24	noon	2 - 2" mortars (in line) handed over to the DTMO. 7" Division and 2 mortars received in exchange. Camps moved to A.29.a.5.7.	
	25	4pm	2 Officers 3 NCO & 38 other ranks sent to TRAMWAY DUMP MORY for duty relieving 58" DAC.	

A.H. Orme
Captain RFA
DTMO 58" DA

30 June 1917.

Army Form C. 2118.

WAR DIARY
INTELLIGENCE SUMMARY.
(Erase heading not required.)

Vol 3

Confidential

War Diary

58th T.M. Bty.

from 1st to 31st July 1917

Army Form C. 2118.

WAR DIARY
or
INTELLIGENCE SUMMARY.
(Erase heading not required.)

Instructions regarding War Diaries and Intelligence Summaries are contained in F. S. Regs., Part II. and the Staff Manual respectively. Title pages will be prepared in manuscript.

Place	Date	Hour	Summary of Events and Information	Remarks and references to Appendices
In the field	July 1917 3rd		Orders received prepare to move	
	4"		X Y Z & V Batteries & D.A.M.O moved by Motor Lorries with 12 : 2 Motors & Stores to FRICOURT CAMP B LINES. V/58 travancashouris from 7nth Aircraft Battery	
	5"		1 Corpl 2 Bomb & 27 other ranks sent to O.C. 58th D.A.C. for fatigues	
	6"	2pm	Inspection of Batteries by B.G.R.A. 58th D.A.	
	7"		3 Officers & 60 other ranks to 58th D/16 for fatigues 1 N.C.O & 10 men to Joan Regrs FRICOURT for fatigues	
	9"		3 Officers & 60 other ranks to 58th D/16 for fatigues 1 N.C.O & 10 men to Joan Regrs FRICOURT for fatigues	
	10"		2/Lieut W. Eden posted to B/290. 2/Lieut R.F.A. from V/58th D/16 2/Lieut R.M. Ruston posted from 6/291st B.W. R.F.A. to V/58th D/16 B.y	
	11"		D.A.M.O & V/58 D/16 B.y moved by motor lorry to Sheet 57 4/29.00 P 33 w 3 3	
	13"		V/58 outspelled 1 Officer & 20 other ranks to Ammunition dump NEUVILLE	
	14"		D.A.M.O & 2 Officers reconnoitre Right Section of our front road in order to selecting possible positions for Trench Mortars X, Y & Z Batteries arrived from COMMECOURT 1 Officer & 30 other ranks supplied for work at ART NEUVILLE and further north	

WAR DIARY
or
INTELLIGENCE SUMMARY.
(Erase heading not required.)

Army Form C. 2118.

Place	Date	Hour	Summary of Events and Information	Remarks and references to Appendices
In the field	16th July		2nd Lieut (Temp Lieut) R C Gudgeon appointed Acting Captain whilst commanding a Heavy Trench Mortar Battery with effect from 9-6-1917	
	17th		2nd Lieut S D Bellamy, appointed Acting Lieutenant whilst commanding a Heavy Trench Mortar Battery with effect from 9-6-1917. 2 men sent to RFA Gunnery instruction for artillery. 1 Officer & 30 other ranks sent to advanced Headquarters 290th Brigade R.F.A. for the purpose of instructing dummy gun positions and to their retention.	
	20"		1 N.C.O. & 12 men sent to 58th D.H.Q. for duty under further orders. 1 N.C.O. & 12 men to advanced H.Q. 291st Brigade R.F.A. for making gun positions, until further orders.	
	21st		1 N.C.O. & 10 men to A.R.P. NEUVILLE	
	22nd		1 N.C.O. & 12 men relief to 291st D.H.Q. advanced H.Q.	
	23rd		1 - 9.45 Heavy Trench Mortar crews on duty under arrangements made since moving & whole platoon round also moving.	
	24		1 Officer & 25 other ranks sent to FOUR WINDS FARM P31 a 0.8 for artillery aerodrome filling in shell holes. 1 N.C.O. & 6 men sent to A.R.P. NEUVILLE under further orders.	
	27"		1 Officer & 20 other ranks to report daily to FOUR WINDS FARM.	

WAR DIARY
or
INTELLIGENCE SUMMARY.
(Erase heading not required.)

Army Form C. 2118.

Place	Date	Hour	Summary of Events and Information	Remarks and references to Appendices
In the field	July 27	8.15	Relief party of 3 NCOs & 17 men despatched to 291st Dvs R.F.A. advanced Headquarters.	
	30	8 a.m	Relief party of 1 NCO & 12 men despatched to 291st Brigade R.F.A. advanced Headquarters.	

W.B. Stevens
Captain RFA
D.T.M.O. 58th D.A.

D.T.M.O.
58TH
DVL. ARTILLERY.
July 31-7-17

WAR DIARY
INTELLIGENCE SUMMARY.
(Erase heading not required.)

Army Form C. 2118.

Vol 4

58th D.I.I.C Brigade

War Diary

— for —

August 1917

WAR DIARY
INTELLIGENCE SUMMARY.
(Erase heading not required.)

August 1917

Place	Date	Hour	Summary of Events and Information	Remarks and references to Appendices
Battle Sheet 51c 1:40,000 P33a 3.3	Aug 1st		N.C.O.s & men attached to 290" Brigade RFA returned to Camp. 9" Division ordered to take over.	
	2nd		N.C.O & men at NEUVILLE dump returned to Camp.	
	3rd		X/58" heavy Mortar handed over to V/9" T.M.B'y. 12 tents handed over to D.T.M.O. 9" division. X & Y/58" moved by Motor Lorries to 51B T 2 & 7 6 and attached to 50" division. (HENIN) Y & Z/58" moved by Motor Lorries to Sheet 51c T 20 2 4 #1 and attached to 21st division. (ST LEGER)	
	4th	8pm	2 Officers, 7 N.C.O.s & 42 men carrying 2" bombs moved to trenches & V/50", X/50", & Z/50".	
	5th		X/58" supplied 1 N.C.O & men to Z/50" for 3 days work. V/58" supplied 4 N.C.O. & 25 men to V/50" carrying trench & protecting parties for 9 and 15 Mortars. Y & Z supplied 1 Officer & 15 men to 21 T.M.B's.	
	6th		ditto	
	7th		ditto	
	8th		V/58" took after 12 mortars of 21 T.M.B. at Sheet 51 B3 W	
	9th		X/58" relief for party employed on the 5" trench Mortars V/58" found 30 reliefs from 6 to installation up to the German front line.	

Army Form C. 2118.

WAR DIARY
INTELLIGENCE SUMMARY.
(Erase heading not required.)

Instructions regarding War Diaries and Intelligence Summaries are contained in F. S. Regs., Part II and the Staff Manual respectively. Title pages will be prepared in manuscript.

Place	Date	Hour	Summary of Events and Information	Remarks and references to Appendices
	10th	8pm	3 N.C.O.s & 25 men from Y/58" to Y/50" position	
	11th		Issued Belle Ruelon details by VI Corps to assist Y/21st N.C.B.G. Y/58th – 4 Norton positions flooded, unable to fire. Considerable firing near positions. Y/58th assisting Y/50" at positions " for 3 days. X/58th " " Z/50 " " " Y/58th positions, enemy firing very considerable especially in vicinity of KNUCKLE AVENUE during morning. Fired 8 rounds from 1st Mortar on to front line silencing GRANATENWERFER. Fired 15 rounds on to front line opposite BEAUMONS LOOP, at position and in the my. two machine gun emplacements, several direct hits on front line observed.	
	12th		2/58" supplied fatigues for Y/58". Y/58" 3 N.C.O.s & 25 men for V/50". Y/58" fired 19 rounds on German front line opposite BEAUMONS LOOP.	
	13th		1 N.C.O. & 1 man from X/58" assisting Z/50" for 3 days. Y/58" fired 19 rounds opposite BEAUMONS LOOP. V/58" 3 N.C.O.s & 25 men for V/50" 1 man of Z/58 wounded.	
	14th		Issued 2/Lt Debnam of V/58" posted to R.F.C. Headquarters for duty as Observer on production of Shoots off strength. V/50".	

Army Form C. 2118.

WAR DIARY
or
INTELLIGENCE SUMMARY.
(Erase heading not required.)

Instructions regarding War Diaries and Intelligence Summaries are contained in F. S. Regs., Part II and the Staff Manual respectively. Title pages will be prepared in manuscript.

Place	Date	Hour	Summary of Events and Information	Remarks and references to Appendices
	15		1 man of Y/58 slightly wounded by shrapnel at WANCOURT.	
			Y/58: 3 x 6.0: 25 men for Y/58 partout	
			Y/58 carried out registration on enemy front line. 3 rounds fired	
	16		ditto for men details cutting	7
			X/58: 3 x 6.0. & 25 men for Y/50	
			V/58: 3 x 6.0 & 25 men for Z/50 for 3 days	
			X/58: 1 x 6.0 & 4 men for Z/50 for 3 days	
	17		V/58: 3 x 6.0 & 25 men for Y/50	
		9.30 am	Y/58 1 position of trench completely blown in & 30 bombs buried.	
		10 am	2nd position blown in every 1st premature causing dug outlet entrance of shrapnel hitting trench immediately before firing	
		12.30 pm	Commenced wire cutting. 71 rounds fired. One premature of 10 "10" round	
			Considerable shelling by long range gun of V/58 & X/58 bombs, one tent of trench badly damaged. Officers nearest but also damaged.	
	18		Y/58: fired 9 rounds at hostile gun position, silencing enemy.	
			V/58: 3 x 6.0: & 25 men to Y/50	
	19		Y/58: ditto	
			V/58: ditto	
	20		X/58: 1 x 6.0 & 4 men for Z/50	
			Y/58: relieved in line	

Army Form C. 2118.

WAR DIARY
or
INTELLIGENCE SUMMARY.
(Erase heading not required.)

Instructions regarding War Diaries and Intelligence Summaries are contained in F. S. Regs., Part II. and the Staff Manual respectively. Title pages will be prepared in manuscript.

Place	Date	Hour	Summary of Events and Information	Remarks and references to Appendices
	Augt 21st		V/58th men back from line. 2/Lieut Campbell & 60 from V/58 out to new area for billeting purposes	
	22nd		V. X. Y. Z/58 moved by DAC transport to Sheet 51.B. M 17c near Headquarters D/58.	
	23rd		I.T.O.O. & 20 men reported to B Echelon 58th D/A for fatigue	
	24th		ditto	
	25		Orders received to prepare to move by rail.	
	26		Artillery D/A to entrain. Battery to entrain Lieut. Foster & O.C. Z/58 returned to duty from Base.	
	27		Entrained at ARRAS Station	
	28	9.30 am	Arrived at Camp 52 HOOGGRAAF map reference BELGIUM Sheet 28 G 26 c 7.9	
	29			
	30	2pm	Landed 10 "Trench warfare camp" near DICKEBUSCH Hutments H 26 d	
	31st			

A.S. Mowat
Captain R.F.A.
O.C. N.O. 58th D.A.

D.T.M.O.
58TH
DIV'L ARTILLERY.

Army Form C. 2118.

WAR DIARY
or
INTELLIGENCE SUMMARY.

(Erase heading not required.)

War Diary
— of —
58 D.A.T.M. ᴮᵈˢ.
September 1917

Army Form C. 2118.

WAR DIARY
INTELLIGENCE SUMMARY.
(Erase heading not required.)

September 1917.

Place	Date	Hour	Summary of Events and Information	Remarks and references to Appendices
Sheet 27 D 22c HERZEELE	Sept. 3rd	8 am	Moved from near DICKEBUSCH to HERZEELE Sheet 27 D 22c to billets No. 79.80.81 & 82.	
	5"	9 am	V/58th Battery attached farmers in camp	
	6"	2 pm	Move to BROWNE HUT CAMP on the POPERINGHE – ELVERDINGHE Road Sheet 28 A 22 d 8.5.	
	8"	6 pm	D.I.M.O. attended conference at R.A.H.Q. Capt. Gudgeon & 2/Lieut Gilboy attended conference at advanced R.A.H.Q. (tanks)	
	9"	9 am	V/58th T.M.Bty proceeded to Camps of 48th T.M.B's for instruction in use of new 9 & 5" Mark II M.L. T.M.	
		4 pm	Party of 2 Officers 3 N.C.O.s & 57 men proceeded in lorries to 290° I. 291ª	
		6 pm	Brigade precautions for fatigue – men not required	
	10"	4 pm	1 – 6 Newton Mortars & Stores taken over from 23rd div. only 4 men required	
			ditto	
			D.I.M.O., Capt. Gudgeon & 2/Lieut Scates proceeded to ST. JULIEN to reconnoitre positions for T.M's	
	11"	4 pm	Party of 2 Officers 3 N.C.O.s & 57 men proceeded in lorries to Battery positions, 4 men only required	
			ditto	
	12"		ditto	

Army Form C. 2118.

WAR DIARY
INTELLIGENCE SUMMARY.
(Erase heading not required.)

Instructions regarding War Diaries and Intelligence Summaries are contained in F. S. Regs., Part II. and the Staff Manual respectively. Title pages will be prepared in manuscript.

Place	Date	Hour	Summary of Events and Information	Remarks and references to Appendices
	Sept 12th	5 pm	V/58th took over 1 Mok II 9.45" Mortar from 40th div at Sheet 28 H20 05.95 & took it to ST JULIEN 1st position Sheet 28 c 12 c, transport from 55th DAC. Party ups in charge.	
	13th	8.30 am	1 Officer & 20 ORs marched to SHELHOEK A.R.P. at A 23 B4.8. to fuze m.s. ammunition	
	14"		ditto	
	15"		V/58" – 9.45" Mortars ready for action. Enemy shell set fire to Wood stack in rear of position. Serious damage caused to gun trucks but no damage to guns itself. 6" Newton Mortar dumpren at the Cross roads ST JULIEN. Work party for SHELHOEK A.R.P. fuzing ammunition	
	16"		SHELHOEK A.R.P. work party	

WAR DIARY

INTELLIGENCE SUMMARY.

(Erase heading not required.)

Army Form C. 2118.

Instructions regarding War Diaries and Intelligence Summaries are contained in F. S. Regs. Part II. and the Staff Manual respectively. Title pages will be prepared in manuscript.

Place	Date	Hour	Summary of Events and Information	Remarks and references to Appendices
	Sept 19th	V/58"	fired 20 rounds at Hostile C.12.d.7.8. 5 effective hits. On the 7" round 8 of the enemy seen to leave the Hostile's disappear over the ridge. 1 prisoner brought in. 2 other targets straightened to in sight of Company and suspected enthustoma near JEWRY FARM, engaged and 5 rounds fired at each	
	20th	V/58"	2 targets engaged - 5 rounds only fired away 10 light. After firing 3 rounds at the 2nd target Ammunition and Gun blown up by a shell apparently a 5.9". Gun lifted about 20 yards. No casualties, detachment under cover.	
	22nd	V/58"	working party to CHEDDAR VILLA.	
	23rd	X/58"	took over 6" Newton Mortar	
	24"	V/58"	Mark III 9.45" Mortar taken up to ST JULIEN position.	

Army Form.C. 2118.

WAR DIARY
or
INTELLIGENCE SUMMARY
(Erase heading not required.)

Instructions regarding War Diaries and Intelligence Summaries are contained in F. S. Regs., Part II. and the Staff Manual respectively. Title pages will be prepared in manuscript.

Place	Date	Hour	Summary of Events and Information	Remarks and references to Appendices
	Sept 25		V/58 reconnoitres Morteru at D.8.c.6.5.55. 4 rounds fired at this target. 2nd round forty effective. Firing Mark III 9 4.5 Howitzer with Mark II charges. 10 rounds fired - CROSS COTTS (1 cwt) Hkonm no right for range but reader for line. X/58 fired a 6" Newton Morters into advance of D7a 75.40. V/58 put a 6" Newton Morter into action at C.12 & B5.60 sheltering Morter at JURY FARM	
	26"		V/58 fired 4 rounds at gun house in direction of BOETHER. Heavy Howitzer gun fire in retaliation from CROSS COTTAGES & gun fired. Enemy mortar premises shell fire	
	27"	5-30 am	X/51 fired 28 rounds from D7a.75.40. V/51 fired 8 rounds at strong target D.I.a.95.25. Accuracy of accuracy not seen & destroyer. Enemy aircraft avoided to take records. V/58 fired 2 rounds at extreme range	
	28"	1pm	Inspection of T.M. Batteries by B.G.R.A. OC.	
		1-30 pm	V/58. party to ST JULIEN to salve guns destroyed by there fire.	
	29"	12 noon	Party of 20 other ranks to 291st Bugades R.F. for fatigue.	

W.S.Moore
Captain B.T.O.
D.I.60. 58th D.I.

30 Sept 1917.

Army Form C. 2118.

WAR DIARY
INTELLIGENCE SUMMARY.
(Erase heading not required.)

War Diary
— of the —
58th Divisional Trench
Mortar Batteries
— for —
October 1917.

Vol 6

D.T.M.O.,
58TH
DIVL. ARTILLERY.
31-10-17

WAR DIARY
—or—
INTELLIGENCE SUMMARY.
(Erase heading not required.)

Army Form C. 2118.

October 1917.

Place	Date	Hour	Summary of Events and Information	Remarks and references to Appendices
Sheet 28 A 22 d & 5	Oct 2nd	4pm	Camp moved from Sheet 28 A 22 d & 5 to Sheet 28 A 28 d 7.2. upon the instructions of the area Commandant.	
	3rd		30 other ranks to LEFT GROUP at LA BELLE ALLIANCE for work with Batteries. 7 other ranks to CENTRE GROUP at HILLTOP ditto. 8 other ranks to RIGHT GROUP at WILSONS FARM. 20 other ranks returned from digging 6 gun positions with 126° Bde A.F.A.	
	4		6 men wounded and 1 man killed of men of above mentioned working party.	
	6		12 men for working party to CENTRE GROUP (D/82 position).	
	9		Camp drains cleaned out & funk holes drained for Camp Commandant.	
	10		20 N.C.O's given to Adjutant 291st Brigade R.F.A. for work at Battery positions digging gun pits.	
	11		Captain Gudgeon R.E. O.C. V/58 M. Battery awarded Military Cross. Bomb. Wratten M.G. V/58 L M. Battery awarded the Military Medal.	

Army Form C. 2118.

WAR DIARY
or
INTELLIGENCE SUMMARY.
(Erase heading not required.)

Instructions regarding War Diaries and Intelligence Summaries are contained in F. S. Regs., Part II. and the Staff Manual respectively. Title pages will be prepared in manuscript.

Place	Date	Hour	Summary of Events and Information	Remarks and references to Appendices
Sheet 28 A 28 d/2	13"		5 N.C.Os and 25 men to Infantry 291st Brigade R.F.A. to assist Batteries at gun positions	
	14"		1 N.C.O & 4 men as relief party working with 291st Brigade R.F.A.	
	17"		6 N.C.Os and men to 290" Brigade R.F.A. to report to R.E. to trench	
	19"		Sergt Bayley G.J. 4/58 J.M. Battery awarded the Military Medal. Bomb. Warburton J. 4/58 J.M. Battery awarded the Military Medal.	
	23rd		1 N.C.O & 6 men as relief for a party working with 291st Brigade R.F.A.	
	28"		ditto	

D.T.M.O.,
58TH
DIVL. ARTILLERY.
Date 31-10-17

A.B. Munro
Captain R.F.A.
D.T.M.O. 58th D.A.

S E C R E T.   W A R   D I A R Y.

58th (LONDON) D. A. C.   -   MONTH ENDING. 31/10/17.

PLACE.	DATE.	HOUR.	SUMMARY OF EVENTS AND INFORMATION.	REMARKS.

"NIL"

J. D. Lloyd Evans.
Lieut:Col.R.F.A.
Comdg. 58th (London) Divnl.Ammn.Column.

TO.
H.Q.R.A.
  58th (London) Division.
31/10/17.

War Diary

of the

58th Divisional Trench Mortar

Batteries

for the

month of November 1917

Army Form C. 2118.

WAR DIARY
or
INTELLIGENCE SUMMARY. 58th Div. T.M. Bs.
November 1917.

(Erase heading not required.)

Place	Date	Hour	Summary of Events and Information	Remarks and references to Appendices
Sheet 28 A.28.d.7.2	Nov 1st	–	N.C.Os and men returned to camp from attachment to 290th & 291st Brigades RFA	
	2nd	–	2 6" Stokes Mortars and one long Mark III 9.45 J.M. and one Mark II J.M. with Mark III carriage handed over to D.J.M.O 1st Division	
	3rd	–	Move by lorries from A.28.d.7.2 to RUMINGHEM (RECQUES Artillery rest area).	
	4th	–	Billets Nos 12-15-16-17-18-& 20.	
	7th	–	GOC RA decided arrangements to remain forthwith between D.J.M.O and Brigade Commanders for the training of T.M. personnel as 18 pr & 4.5 Howitzer Runners.	
	10th	–	1-4.5 How. taken over from D/290. and 1-18 pr from B/291st Gun and Howitzer returned to Batteries. Warning order to move received.	
	11th	–		
	12th	–	V Z & X Batteries moved by lorries from RUMINGHEM to LONGFOSSE and billeted for night. Y Battery unable to move owing to insufficient supply of lorries	
	13th	–	V Z & X Batteries arrived at LONGVILLERS. 2 lorries sent back for Y/58 Battery(part rations)	
	15th	–	Y/58 T.M. Battery arrived at LONGVILLERS.	

Army Form C. 2118.

WAR DIARY
or
INTELLIGENCE SUMMARY.
(Erase heading not required.)

November 1917.

Place	Date	Hour	Summary of Events and Information	Remarks and references to Appendices
	16"		—	
	17"		2 - 18 pdr guns and 1 - 4.5" Howitzer and 3 Instructors received from 290 & 291st B.F.A. Brigades for instructional purposes.	
	30"	10 am	Inspection of Batteries and sheds by G.O.C. R.A.	

A.S.Hunter,
Captain R.F.A.,
D.T.M.O. 58th Div.

D.T.M.O.
58TH
DIVL. ARTILLERY.
No.
Date 30-11-17

Vol 8

58th Divisional Trench
Mortar Batteries

War Diary — for —
December 1917

D.T.M.O.
58TH
DIV. ARTILLERY

WAR DIARY
— or —
INTELLIGENCE SUMMARY.

Army Form C. 2118.

December 1917

(Erase heading not required.)

Place	Date	Hour	Summary of Events and Information	Remarks and references to Appendices
LONGVILLERS	1917 Dec 3rd		Warning order received to prepare to move by road to II Corps area.	
			Two 18 pr guns and one 4.5 Howitzer returned to 291st and 290th Bdes R.H. respectively.	
	4th Jan		8 lorries reported. Move from LONGVILLERS to THIEMBRONNE area. Billets for night of 4/5 at FAQUEMBERQUE.	
	5 Sun		Move off to ST. MOMELIN. Billets for night 5/6 in ST. MOMELIN.	
	6 11am		Move on to ZERMEZEELE area. Billets for night 6/7 at HARDIFORT.	
	7 8am		D.H.Q. & 2 Officers proceeded to T.M. demonstration at Second Army T.M. School.	
	8th		Move on to HAMOEK area. Billets at camp Sheet 28.A.28.5.9	
			Order received to move to camp at Sheet 28.B.15.c.4.f. (Fields Camp)	
	10th		Moved by Motor Lorries to new Camp.	
	11		Work of Salvage of Guns taken over from D.T.M.O. 18th Division	
	12th		2 Officers 5 N.C.Os & 35 men proceeded to Oost at Canal Bank to commence work of Salvage.	

WAR DIARY
or
INTELLIGENCE SUMMARY.
(Erase heading not required.)

December 1917.

Army Form C. 2118.

Place	Date	Hour	Summary of Events and Information	Remarks and references to Appendices
Sheet 28 B5 c.4.7.	Dec 12/13		1 Sergeant 3 Gunners sent to 58th Reserve Gun Park at B28 c.99.65 for duty.	
			Five 6" Newton Mortars and two 9.45" Mortars taken III taken over from 18th Division at B28 Central (TROISTOURS)	
	14		Coy to move from B15 c.4.7 to B28 central (TROISTOURS)	
	16		D.160 of Seed Cartes reconnoitred POELCAPPELLE a.m. reconnoitring district for possible Trench Mortar positions. V/58th T.M. Battery (made up to War establishment from Newton Batteries) proceeded to Fourth Army Trench Mortar School of Instruction on a course.	
	17		1 Officer & 7 others ranks proceeded to Second Army Trench Mortar School of Instruction	
			Two 6" Newton Mortars sent to D.A.D.O.S. 58th Division for transfer to 35th Division	
	22nd		Two 6" Newton Mortars taken over from 18th Division which had been taken away without corps sanction.	

WAR DIARY
INTELLIGENCE SUMMARY.

December 1917

Army Form C. 2118.

Place	Date	Hour	Summary of Events and Information	Remarks and references to Appendices
Sheet 28	Dec 23rd		Guns for LICHFIELD A.R.P. completed each alternate night.	
B 28 central	24th	6pm	Train of 4.5" Ammunition unloaded at LICHFIELD A.R.P.	
	30		G.O.C., R.A. inspected camp and Mortars.	

S.A. Nash
Lieut R.F.A.
4/DTMO 58th Division

D.T.M.O.
58TH
R.L. ARTILLERY
Date 31.12.17

No 9

A War Diary

of the

58th Divisional French Mortar Batteries

January 1918.

D.T.M.O.,
58TH
DIVL. ARTILLERY.
January
Dated 31-1-18.

Army Form C. 2118.

WAR DIARY
or
INTELLIGENCE SUMMARY.
(Erase heading not required.)

58 Divisional
French Western Battalion

January 1918

Instructions regarding War Diaries and Intelligence Summaries are contained in F.S. Regs., Part II. and the Staff Manual respectively. Title pages will be prepared in manuscript.

Place	Date 1918	Hour	Summary of Events and Information	Remarks and references to Appendices
Sheet 28 B 28 central	Jan 3rd		58th Russian relieved Sheet 28 B.28 43 working parties on Battery position	
TROIS TOURS	4"		Lieut Billson & party relieved of storage of guns	
	5"		4 Officers & 22 attached proceeded to Second Army Tunnel Workshop	
	6"		of Instruction for course from 6" to 19" January 1918	
			V/58" F.M. Bty returned from Lewis Lung F.M. School Instructor at VAUX	
			AMIENOIS and 1 Officer and other ranks returned from Second	
			Army F.M. School at LEULINGHEM	
	9"		D.H.Q. & J.H.Q. 35" Division pursued POELCAPPELLE with a view	
			to finding positions Tunnels Worked positions	
	12		Party returned from work at forward Battery positions	
	14		Give C Newton Morters and Vier 9"2 long Morters interviewed	
			by 35" Divisional Artillery	
	19"		2 Officers & 23 other ranks proceeded Tewksbury F.M. School	
			at VAUX en AMIENOIS	
	20"		Camp moved from Sheet 28 B 28 central (TROIS TOURS) to Sheet 28	
			A.22.d.7.2 Boeming Camp	

WAR DIARY
or
INTELLIGENCE SUMMARY.

Army Form C. 2118.

January 1918

(Erase heading not required.)

Place	Date	Hour	Summary of Events and Information	Remarks and references to Appendices
2nd A 22 d 7.2	20		4 Officers & 22 O.R's who returned from S. Army G.O Bde at Second Army T.M. School.	
	23	12:30 p.m.	Entrained at PROVEN en rte for VILLERS-BRETONNEUX	
	24	2 a.m.	arrived detraining station.	
			Move by Lorry to HAMELET - billets	
	28	6 a.m.	X, Y, & Z Batteries move by Lorry to CHAUNY - billets	
	29	8 a.m.	V/58 Battery move by Lorry to CHAUNY - billets	
	31		Lieut Hamlett left for Fourth Army T.M. School for Asst of Instructor at the School	
	30		2 Officers & 50 O.R's came to relieve us in the 58 A.R.T.	

A.R. Horner
Captain RFA o/c
O.T.M.O. 58th Div. Arty

D.T.M.O.
58TH
DIVL. ARTILLERY.
31-1-18

Vol 10

5⁸ᵗʰ Div: Trench Mortar
Batteries

War Diary

for

February 1918.

WAR DIARY
INTELLIGENCE SUMMARY

February 1918

58th Divl T.M.Bs

Army Form C. 2118.

Place	Date	Hour	Summary of Events and Information	Remarks and references to Appendices
CHAUNY	3rd 5th		1 Officer & 20 other ranks detailed to take over 58th ARP No 2 from 5th Army Brigade RHA	
	6th		Orders received from RAHQ for re-organization of TMBs. V/58 and X/58th M.Bys personnel transferred to X/58 and Y/58 TMBs to make these Batteries up to the new Establishment	
	8th		Re-organization completed	
	10th		6 Newton Mortars received from DADOS 58th Div	
	13th		O i/c & Officers reconnoitre Divisional Park	
	14th		ditto	
	18th		1/Lieut Johnson posted to 5th I.T.M.Bs from DAC. 1 Sergt & 1 Corpl & 3 Gunners surplus to new Establishment to be posted to V/III -Corps- M.L. Battery	
	20th		Captn Gueogon RE6 and Batman posted to V/Mortars 1 to B14 12 Gas ejectors 6" M.L. TMs received from DADOS	
	21st		1/Lt Vernon S.C. posted to 58th D.A.C.	
	22nd		1/Lt R. Mc Ruston posted to South Army I.T.M. School as Instructor.	

Army Form C. 2118.

WAR DIARY
INTELLIGENCE SUMMARY.
(Erase heading not required.)

58th Divr T.M.B.
February 1918

Place	Date	Hour	Summary of Events and Information	Remarks and references to Appendices
CHAUNY	Feb. 22		Lieut S.E. Yorke MC and Lieut J.D. Bellow promoted to ranks of Captains whilst commanding a Medium T.M. Battery.	
	24		Personnel relieved by DAC Personnel at ARP. No 1 and 2. Work of getting T.M. to "Yorlas" took action commenced.	

A.R. Mannin
Captain RFA
O.C No 58th D.T.M.B.

D.T.M.O.,
58TH
DIVL. ARTILLERY.
No.
Date 28-2-18

14

58th Divisional Trench Mortar
Batteries

Vol II

War Diary

for the

month of March 1918.

WAR DIARY or INTELLIGENCE SUMMARY

58th Div: Arty. H.Q. March 1918. Army Form C. 2118.

(Erase heading not required.)

Place	Date	Hour	Summary of Events and Information	Remarks and references to Appendices
CHAMNY	1st		Lieut. M.E. Young Hstarted to the Brahsford posted to IHQ from 291st Brigade RFA	
	4		IHQ Conference at III Corps T.M School BEAUMONT on BEINE	
			Eight 2" M.L Mortars returned to DADOS 58th Divt. after instruction for 1st ORA	
	6		IHQ emplacements in course of preparation at	
			Sheet 70D NW. H 15d 38 40 2 mortars	
			Sheet 66c SW. T 29b. 30 85 2 "	
			T 22c 40 15 2 "	
			Sheet 70D NW. H 16 75 2 "	
			B 27c 3 4 2 "	
			B 27a 7 7 2 "	
			B 27a 5 5 2 "	
	10		Alternative emplacements at " "	
			4 wooden sub. beds for 6" Newton Mortars received from III Corps workshops	
	11		Lieut. E. de Bradsford & one N.C.O sent to 13" Course at III Corps Obs School.	
	12		160 rounds 6" T.M Ammunition taken over to Regt. group positions	

Army Form C. 2118.

WAR DIARY
or
INTELLIGENCE SUMMARY.
(Erase heading not required.)

Instructions regarding War Diaries and Intelligence Summaries are contained in F. S. Regs., Part II. and the Staff Manual respectively. Title pages will be prepared in manuscript.

Place	Date	Hour	Summary of Events and Information	Remarks and references to Appendices
CHAUNY	13th		170 rounds of 6" T.M. Ammn taken up to Left group positions	
			60 rounds of 6" T.M. Ammn taken up to 10" Right group positions	
	18th		Instructions from BM 58th D.A. to form alternative positions to be able to	
			shoot at the BUTTES du ROUY at 800 yards range	
			350 rounds of T.M. Ammn taken up to Right group positions	
	19th		Positions reconnoitred at H 1.a 37/65, Sheet 70D N.W.	
	21st		Positions subjected to heavy bombardment. 4 Horses — Left Group	
			captured by enemy. Observers saved. Corporal I.D. McClean & J. Beard	
			N.C. Young and 2 N.C.O's missing.	
			2 mortars and bases at H 15 & 38.40 withdrawn to transport lines	
	22nd		Situation normal on Right group front.	
	23rd		Right group subjected to faulty Lacry shelling by 5.9° and gas shell	
			2 mortars nr dumbar road destroyed by enemy shell fire B29.	
			J.M. Headquarters moved from CHAUNY to OGNES and then to QUIERZY	
			2 motors of which the parts had not been blown in salved from AMIGNY-ROUY.	
	24th		Move to BICHANCOURT and then on to BOURGUIGNON	
	25th		Move to BLERANCOURT (3 G.S. Wagons on loan from Q.I.6)	

WAR DIARY
INTELLIGENCE SUMMARY.
(Erase heading not required.)

Army Form C. 2118.

Place	Date	Hour	Summary of Events and Information	Remarks and references to Appendices
BLERANCOURT	26		Moved from BLERANCOURT to AH 4 KG a position unknown to BLERANCOURT.	
	25"		Over 200 rounds fired from Battery position on Station trestiers at Enemy.	
			request of Infantry commander. Gas bombardment from 3 am till 6am. LE	
	27"		Move from BLERANCOURT to AUDIGNICOURT & ST MESNIL	
	28"		D.T.M.O carried out reconnaissance	
	29"		ditto	
	30"		12 Observers sent off assist in taking 2 guns of 6/291st Brigade RFA	

A B Munn
Captain RFA
D.T.M.O 58th D.A

D.T.M.O.,
58TH
DIVL. ARTILLERY.
No. 31-3-18
Date

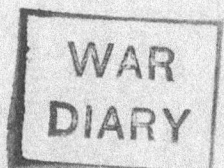

58th DIVISIONAL ARTILLERY TRENCH MORTAR BATTERIES.

A P R I L

1 9 1 8

Vol 12

War Diary

of the

5th Divl. Arty Trench Mortar
Batteries

for April 1918.

Army Form C. 2118.

WAR DIARY
or
INTELLIGENCE SUMMARY.
(Erase heading not required.)

April 1918.

Instructions regarding War Diaries and Intelligence Summaries are contained in F. S. Regs., Part II. and the Staff Manual respectively. Title pages will be prepared in manuscript.

Place	Date	Hour	Summary of Events and Information	Remarks and references to Appendices
AUDIGNICOURT				
LE MESNIL	1st	—	—	
	2nd	4 p.m.	Left LE MESNIL and proceeded to CHEVILLECOURT	
	3rd	10 a.m.	Left CHEVILLECOURT proceeded to railhead at VILLERS-COTTERETS	
	4th	3 p.m.	Entrained at VILLERS-COTTERETS and LONGPONT	
	5th	9 a.m.	Detrained at BACOUEL and LONGUEAU	
			Marched to BOUTERILLIE and CAGNY.	
	6th		D.J.H.O conference with 16" D.T.M.O	
	7th		All Officers and personnel placed at disposal of C.O. 58" Div. whilst not in action. 2 Batteries proceeded to GLISY turning Guns & gun & stores at BOUTERILLIE	
	8th		Lt. gun ejecting & blade with heaving & elevating gear drawn from D.A.D.O.S. 58" Div.	
			D.J.H.O proceeded to 1" D.A.C.Q at BOVES concerning instructions as for the position for 6" J.H.O when ammunition supply available.	
	10th			
	11"		1 Officer & 3 Methowands issued 39" D.T.M.Q to lates up ammunition to positions	
	12"		— ditto —	
	13"		D.J.H.O received instructions as to defensive position	

WAR DIARY
INTELLIGENCE SUMMARY.
(Erase heading not required.)

April 1918

Place	Date	Hour	Summary of Events and Information	Remarks and references to Appendices
	16		D.116.O.3. O.6.x & y.1.16.D. carried out reconnaissance of Dump Talbot	
	17		All Officers and men withdrawn from dump work	
	18		4 mortars taken up to VILLERS BRETTONNEUX and put in action at O.35.6.7.2. and O.35.6.6.4. (A lot of gas shells used by enemy here)	
	19	9am	Guns ready for action	
		3/10	Guns withdrawn for shore full of gas	
	20		D.J.16.O of 20° Division took over part of line	
			2 mortars taken up to T.18.L.8.8. (GENTELLES)	
	21		160 rounds Ammunition taken up to T.18 & 88	
	22		2 mortars taken over from 61st D.J.16.O at U.16.c.88 and U.29.a.35	
			HANGARD 62 rounds fired from U.16.c.88 and U.29.a.35 Ammunition & component parts taken over, very wet.	
	23		2 mortars handed over to 61st D.J.16.O in exchange for those taken over in the line.	
	25		D.J.16.O submitted list of proposed emplacements near GENTELLES to OORA 2 Mortars moved from T.18.6.88. to T.18.x.0.3. Montgomellard Evening	

WAR DIARY
INTELLIGENCE SUMMARY.
(Erase heading not required.)

Army Form C. 2118.

April 1918.

Place	Date	Hour	Summary of Events and Information	Remarks and references to Appendices
	26		4 motors received from D.A.D.O.S. 58th Div. to replace.	
	27		58th D.A. Group Order No 128 directed to withdraw from area all 6" Trench Mortars. Mortars withdrawn as directed.	
	28		Orders received from H.Q.R.A. to move at 10.40 am 29 April to a billetting area round CROUY — to ST PIERRE.	
	29		Proceeded by Route March to ST PIERRE and ST ACHEUL — Abbey — and FRENCIERES and LONGPRÉ & COQUEREL	
	30		Proceeded by Route March to FRENCIERES. Billets in FRENCIERES.	

A. M. [signature]
Captain R.F.A.
D.T.M.O. 58th D.A.

D.T.M.O.,
58TH
DIVL. ARTILLERY.
No. ....
Date 30. 4. 1918

Vol 13

58th Divisional Trench
Mortar Batteries R.A.

War Diary

for the

month of May 1918

58th D.L.
T.M. B's

Army Form C. 2118.

WAR DIARY
or
INTELLIGENCE SUMMARY.
(Erase heading not required.)

May 1918.

Place	Date	Hour	Summary of Events and Information	Remarks and references to Appendices
FRANCIERES	1st	-	In rest. Training Programme.	
	4th		Warning orders from H.Q.R.A. - Prepare to move	
	13th		Notice received that G.O.C., R.A. Fourth Army wanted inspect Divl Artillery.	
	15th		D.T.M.O. proceeded to WARLOY with Brigade Majors.	
			58th Divl Arty order No 131 to move received	
U24 d 4.3 Sheet 57.P.	16		Move by Lorries to WARLOY-BAILLON - Billets in schools near Church.	
	17		6 Guns and 540 rounds 6" T.M. Ammunition taken over from D.T.M.O. 47	
			Division Positions of guns W.20.c.85.40 - W.20.d.25.55 - W.20.c.80.70 - W.20.c.65.80	
			W.15.c.1.1. Emplacements under construction W.20.c.70.20 and W.15.c.10.13.	
	18		6 guns handed over to D.T.M.O. 47 Divn in exchange for 6 staked over our line	
	19		Shoot carried out on Sunken roads & trenches in W.15.c. Enemy garrison W.20.c.	
	20th		Fired at junction of sunken road trench and track in W.22.c.3.1 and trench in	
			W.22.c.9.3	
	21st		ditto W.15 B.9.9 W.21.d W.27.c 5.8	
			ditto for full positions (rear) in V.24 c.3 d	
			D.T.M.O reconnoitred for new positions taken up to new position 2 weeks	
			4 mortars and 80 rounds composed of Ammunition on implements begun.	

Army Form C. 2118.

WAR DIARY
INTELLIGENCE SUMMARY.
(Erase heading not required.)

May 1918

Place	Date	Hour	Summary of Events and Information	Remarks and references to Appendices
WARLOY	May 22nd		20 rounds fired on trenches in W.21.c. — W.15.d. southern road engaged	
			100 rounds of "Mustard" gas shells fell on & around BOUZINCOURT	
	23rd		2 mortars in V.24.c.5.3 ready to fire. Two small dumps were reported by the Infantry to have been "put up" by enemy. Position constructed at W.14.d. 7.9.	
			Enemy fired about 200 rounds (7mm gas shells) in the neighbourhood of V.30.a & V.24.d.A.N.3.	
	24th		Wires rough engaged on W.27.c. & 9 & W.27.d.O.6. 2 more trenches at V.24.d.2.3 ready to fire	
	25th		21 rounds fired on several types Cylinders of 60 Infantry. Several dumps hit. Enemy trenches W.27.a. were engaged.	
	26th		upon enemy trenches were observed. Road's trenches W.27.a were engaged.	
			O.I.C. Dismounted Brigade took over with 174th Brigade Staff today	
			Bursts of free rounds each fired on Sunken road at W.22.a.1.7 and W.16.9.2 am	
			Quarry W.27.c.2.8 and trench W.27.c.6.8.	
	27th		Bouzincourt heavily shelled by enemy. Fired a number at W.27.d.1.5 from W.22.c.1.7	
			About 100 rounds gas shell (mustard gas) at about W.20	
	28th		21 rounds fired at Orchard W.21.A.3.5 trench cross road W.27.a.7.2	
			Trench junction W.27.c. 4.9 & trench 27.c. 3.9	
			Enemy Artillery very active	

WAR DIARY
— or —
INTELLIGENCE SUMMARY.
(Erase heading not required.)

Army Form C. 2118.

May 1918

Place	Date	Hour	Summary of Events and Information	Remarks and references to Appendices
WARLOY	May 29th	3pm to 4pm	In co-operation with the Heavy Howitzers. Observed fire as the following targets:- Trench junction W.22.a.1.6 - Sunken road W.22.a.3.2 - Brickworks W.22.a.4.4 - Sunken room W.22.a.5.d - junction of trench road W.27.a.7.2 - Trench junction W.27.b no 5 - point W.27.b.30.90 - point W.27.c.20.70 - Haystacks W.27.d.10.10. & Sunken room.	
	30th		Enemy retaliated with a few rounds at W.15.c.3.1 and at W.20.d.9.2. Harrasing targets on W.27.b.7.30 and W.22.a engaged during the night.	
	31st		Fired 20 rounds on sunken road & trenches in W.15.d. & W.21.b. 5 rounds on trench junction W.21.c. and 10 rounds on Quarry W.27.c.	

D.T.M.O.,
58TH
DIVL. ARTILLERY.
31st May 1918

A. B. Munro
Captain R.F.A.
Commanding 58th Div. Arty. T.M.B.

58th Divisional French
Mortar Batteries R.A.

War Diary

for

the month of June 1918

Vol 14

58' D.T.M. Bs

Army Form C. 2118.

WAR DIARY
INTELLIGENCE SUMMARY
(Erase heading not required)

June 1918

Place	Date	Hour	Summary of Events and Information	Remarks and references to Appendices
WARLOY U.24.d.6.3.	1st			
	2nd		18" D.T took over tactical command of Bn Bty.	
			D.T.M.O arranged with 18" D.T.M.O exchange of Batteries positions	
	3rd		18" D.T.M.O took over 6" Mortars — lent at W.20.c.5.2. W.15.c. W.14.d. &	
			V.24.c.y.d. also 341 rds Ammunition	
	4th		58" D.T.M.O. took over reserve position in HENENCOURT WOOD	
			V.26.d. and 480 rds Ammunition	
	5th		10 Mortars taken over from 18" D.T.M.O in exchange for their handed	
			over positions	
	7th		to reserve position at V.26.b handed over to 18" D.T.M.O. 3 words TM G	
	8th		Orders received to move on 9th June.	
	9th		Mine frames & sand bags handed over to 47" L.T.M Bs.	
			Move by 5 lorries to LONGPRÉ near AMIENS.	
	12"		D.T.M.O. to IX Survey Corps for reconnoitre	
	13"		Training programme	
	14" 18"		ditto	

WAR DIARY
INTELLIGENCE SUMMARY.
(Erase heading not required.)

Army Form C. 2118.

Place	Date	Hour	Summary of Events and Information	Remarks and references to Appendices
LONGPRE	18th		D/160 proceeded to WARLOY to arrange retirement with 47th D.T.M.O.	
		10 pm	Orders to move received	
	19th	9 am	Move from LONGPRE to WARLOY by 5 buses	
WARLOY	20th		6.6 mortars taken over in the line by x 55th T.M. By. from 47th T.M. By. at E.7.b, E.13.a & D.18.d. By Headquarters at E.13.a.25.50	
	21st		80 rds fired on enemy front line, front junctions & targets observed with good effect	
	22nd		25 of new mortar from 1st sent to coast B/291st Infantry D.T.M.O. reconnoitred & photographs to B.O.R.4 on registered issued	
			position for the defence of LAVIEVILLE Over 100 rounds were fired on enemy trenches & strong point, Crew By mortar active with 20th 25 5.9's	
	23rd		2 shorts carried out with 3 guns upon enemy trenches on E.8.c, E.11.c, E.13.d	
			By. Two guns were shelled by enemy from 3.15 to 4.30 p.m.	
	24th		90 rds fired on enemy trenches at E.14.a, E.19.b & E.14.a (4 guns firing) By. H.Qrs shelled with 5.9 from 7.30 am till 9.15 am	

WAR DIARY or INTELLIGENCE SUMMARY

Army Form C. 2118.

Place	Date	Hour	Summary of Events and Information	Remarks and references to Appendices
WARLOY	June 25		Position for wagon lines & defence of LAVIEVILLE drawn & dumps	
			20 rds fired on enemy battery junction on E14c E20a E14a E13d	
			and E19d. B.O. to R.A. visited Bn positions	
			Enemy shelled E14c with 15 rds Hy 77.	
	26	6h	Fired 30 rds on E14a x & E8a 35.80 and 40 rds on T.M. position by	
			File roads at E14c 0 70.60 in retaliation (alleged of infantry) Hitherto 7M	
		10.45	About 25 gas shells fell in vicinity of Sig 50	
	27	5pm	50 rds fired in retaliation on enemy front line system between	
		4pm	E8c 75.25 and 13d 4 95.15 negatives at the request of the Infantry	
	28		Enemy MG at E13 & 95.15 negatives at the request of the Infantry	
			60 rds fired at enemy front line system	
	29	1pm	Hdqrs established at 291st BHn returned. Side fired at hostile M.G. at E13c 95.10	
			40 rds fired on enemy trenches & trench W. of E14c 570 - E13d 50.45 - E8a 80.30 & E14c 23.05	Bridges
	30		Shots were caused into 5 guns on the following targets - E9c 80.25 - E14c a 80.90 E14c 25.70 E14c 15.0 85/E13.d 90.25	
		9.35pm	Co-operated with Artillery gp of 69 - 60 rds fired on E13 d 30.30 - E 13d 65.00	

A.B. Morris.
Captain RFA
O/C 260 58 DA

D.T.M.O.
58TH
DIV. ARTILLERY.

30-6-1918

58th Div Arty Trench Mortar Batteries.

War Diary
for
July 1918.

YA 15

D.T.M.O.
58TH
DIVL. ARTILLERY.
31-7-1918

WAR DIARY or INTELLIGENCE SUMMARY

Army Form C. 2118.

5" Div: T No 9.
R.A.

July 1918.

Place	Date	Hour	Summary of Events and Information	Remarks and references to Appendices
WARLOY	July 1st		Commenced new position for defence of LAVIEVILLE	
		5.15 am	The following targets engaged. Trenches at E19c.40.90 — Trenches E19c.85.90. TM at E8c	
		6.30 pm		
		7.30 pm	80.25 Salvo at E14w.80.90. Quarry at E14c.25.65. M.G. E14w.95.10 Crossroads E15a.15.05	
		8 pm		
			M.G. E2c.60.05 and Crossroads E13d.90.25	
	2nd	5.30pm	10 rds fired at T.M. E8c.70.90	
	3rd		Q1 NCO proceeded to leave. Captain Abfalls acting O.C. NCO	
		3.50am	40 rds fired on hostile T.M. Crossroads & Quarry	
		6.50		
	4th	3.10	Co-operated with flanks divisions — 100 rds fired. Hostile defences TM's arr. se	
		10.15(-)	Robbery shoot on TM's — E13d. E20a. E14w carried out on defences E13d. E14w. E8d	
	5th	3.10	Bombardment for our raid carried out on defences on E13d E14w E14w in retaliation	
		6.4.10am		
		2.40pm		
		9.20pm		
	6th	1.15am	160 rds fired on T.M's E14w E13d Quarry E14w — in retaliation	
		10pm	130 rds fired at hostile TM: Quarry defences — E13d. E14w. E14w. E19c.	
	7th	10.15am	16 rds fired on Quarry Crossroads MG trenches in E14w E13d and E19c	
		8.10pm	60 rds fired in retaliation on T.M's in E14w and E14c	
	8th	2pm	30 rds fired on Quarry on E14c.25.65 & trench E19c.70.50	
	9th	6.30pm	70 rds fired on T.M's E14c & E20d and E13d	

Army Form C. 2118.

WAR DIARY
or
INTELLIGENCE SUMMARY.
(Erase heading not required.)

Instructions regarding War Diaries and Intelligence Summaries are contained in F. S. Regs., Part II. and the Staff Manual respectively. Title pages will be prepared in manuscript.

Place	Date 1918	Hour	Summary of Events and Information	Remarks and references to Appendices
Bus	July 10	6pm	59 rds fired on Groups C Hostile T.M. alerted tanks & transport Elhc	
	11"	3.30	67 rds fired on Groups Hostile T.M. B & D and Tanks & transport Elhc, E13d	
	12"	6pm	60 rds fired on Groups A.B.C.D Hostile T.M's and tanks/transport in Elhc	
	13"	3pm	65 rds fired on Groups J transport E8c, E8a, E19a &	
	14"	3pm	65 rds fired on Targets B Tanks, Transport in E13d, E14c, E19c &	
	15"	5hr	70 rds fired in wire trenches & earthworks in E13d, E14c	
	16	2.30pm	130 rds fired on Earthworks E13d, M.G. Emp, wire in E13d	
	17"	7.30	100 rds fired in Groups J and G TMs and wire in E13d	
	18"	11.30	80 rds fired on wire trenches in E13d, E13c, and Groups B hostile TMs	
	19"	3pm	103 rds fired on several targets	
	20"	6.30	82 rds fired on Groups A and D and tanks & transport E14c & E13d	
			4 Officers & 52 other ranks left for course of instruction at the Faults	
			Army T.M. School. MILLY FLIRBEAUCOURT	
	21"	7am	52 rds fired on Mortars Elyb, Quarry Ehcb	
	22nd		N3 D.M.G.'s Headquarters moved up to Quarry in D4c 2.4	
	22nd	10	N3 rds fired on Groups A & B and Tanks & transport in E13d	
Duc 24				

WAR DIARY
or
INTELLIGENCE SUMMARY.
(Erase heading not required.)

Army Form C. 2118.

Place	Date	Hour	Summary of Events and Information	Remarks and references to Appendices
	1917 July	p.m.		
Duc 2A	23rd	3.30	6 rds fired on Groups A,B,&J. Hostile T.M.s ow. co-operation M.G. E.14	
	24"	3.	9 rds fired on Group J and Bank and wire E.14.c.a.+ E.13 d	
	25"	6.15½	88 rds fired on Group Ram & Hostile T.M. and trenches in E.14.a & E.19.c	
		3 pm	O.T.60 & 5th Australian Div. called in taking over of Montauban new line	
	26"	12 noon	O.T.60 proceeded to HEILLY in making over. 58th D.A. order No. 144	
	27"	12.15 pm	60 rds fired on Quarry E.14.c & Groups J and R T.M.s	
	28"	11 am	10 rds fired on Quarry E.14.c at request of Infantry	
	28"	9 am	46 rds fired on Groups "B", "R" & J harassing & in retaliation	
	29"	12.45 pm	Co-operation with 5th Australian Division - Hosts fires on Quarry E.14.c and trench of trenches in K.1d and K.2c. as ordered by 58th D.A. Order No. 146	
			Words fired (harassing & retaliatory fire) on hostile T.M. E.14.c, Quarry, &c	
	29"		dM	
	30"		To do hew dM	
	31	12.5 a.m.	58th D.A. order No. 147 on relief of 58th Div. Arty by 25th Div. Arty received	

Alfred C. Ball
Captain R.G.A.
O.T.60 58th D.A.

58th Divl. Artillery

58th DIVISIONAL TRENCH MORTAR OFFICER,

AUGUST 1918.

58th Divisional Trench Mortar Batteries.

War Diary for August 1918.

WAR DIARY
INTELLIGENCE SUMMARY
August 1918. Army Form C. 2118.

(Erase heading not required.)

Instructions regarding War Diaries and Intelligence Summaries are contained in F.S. Regs., Part II. and the Staff Manual respectively. Title pages will be prepared in manuscript.

Place	Date Augt	Hour	Summary of Events and Information	Remarks and references to Appendices
	1st		D.T.M.O. 25" Dn Arty took over 5 Mortars & Ammunition forward positions and 6 reserve position (LAVIEVILLE) and Ammunition. H.Q. removed from Quarry in D.4.C.2.4. to 1 Main Street, WARLOY.	
	2nd		Took over 10 - 6" Mortars from 25" D.T.M.O. in exchange for those handed over.	
	5"		Min by Cny from WARLOY to Bellos in PONT NOYELLES	
	6"		Durward fwd for forward T.M. position by D.T.M.O. reconnoitred B/291st Bde R.F.A. for pulling mortars setting into at J.3 d & c.3	
		1pm	1 Capt & 12 men report to B/291st Bde R.F.A. for pulling mortars setting into at J.3 d & c.3	
	8"		11 other ranks to advanced H.Q. R.A. as working party friday	
			1 Officer & 35 other ranks to 290" Bde forward H.Q. as forward working party.	
	10"		1 Officer & 12 other ranks to ABBEVILLE for remounts	
	11"		Capt Simeons proceeded up the line to bring back German T.M. for the Y.O.C.	
	12"		14 other ranks to advanced H.Q. R.A. working party	
	15		1 Officer & 17 other ranks to A.R.P. Chipilly for duty.	

Army Form C. 2118.

WAR DIARY
or
INTELLIGENCE SUMMARY.
(Erase heading not required).

Instructions regarding War Diaries and Intelligence Summaries are contained in F. S. Regs., Part II. and the Staff Manual respectively. Title pages will be prepared in manuscript.

Place	Date 1918 Aug	Hour	Summary of Events and Information	Remarks and references to Appendices
PONT-NOYELLES	19	—	D.T.M.O. 3rd Australian division is taking over. Officers & other ranks returned from attachment to Ontario.	
	20		D.T.M.O. to forward R.I.E.9.	
	24		G.O.C., R.A. inspected detachments at gun drill	
	25		Move by lorry to HEILLY Sheet 62D J 2 a 1.2.	
	26		1 Officer & 20 other ranks to ARP K 13 d to takeover from 50'DA 1 Officer & 20 other ranks to ARP K 7 central ditto.	
	27		1 Officer to ARP E 18 central.	

A.R.Horton
Captain RFA
D.T.M.O. 58'D.I.

D.T.M.O.
50TH
DIVL. ARTILLERY.
No.
Date 31-8-1918

War Diary
of the
59th Divn. T.M. Bs. R.A.
for the
month of September 1918.

58 D.T.M.B.

WAR DIARY
or
INTELLIGENCE SUMMARY.
(Erase heading not required.)

September 1918 Army Form C. 2118.

Place	Date	Hour	Summary of Events and Information	Remarks and references to Appendices
HEILLY	3rd		2 6" Mortars sent to Workshops MONTIERES for fitting of new spares attachment	
	4		Instructions received from ADRA for the collection of all German Light T.Ms and Ammunition in the Divisional area	
14d/72	6		Move from HEILLY to HAUT ALLAINES 14d 72	
	7		2 mortars fitted with spare attachments at D.15.a. 200' D/W RFA HQ 10' S in close commuication with 173rd Inf Bde	
	9		Orders to get as many TMs into action as possible before mid-nights	
	10		2 mortars got into action to bombard EPEHY 30 rds per ...	
	11		5.7/4cm Light German Minnenwerfer & 282 rds Ammn. taken Ronaelo	
	12	5pm	Move to NURLU for night	
E7c 22	13		Move to LIERAMONT E7c 22	
			2 additional 6" Mortars & 1 76cm German T.M. taken up & put into action at 1. 6" & 1 7.6cm E12 a 40.40 — 1 76 minn written at " 1. 6" & 1. 6" minn at E12 a 50.42 & 1 E12 a 60.35 2 Mortars taken up at ...	

WAR DIARY or INTELLIGENCE SUMMARY

Army Form C. 2118.

(Erase heading not required.)

Place	Date	Hour	Summary of Events and Information	Remarks and references to Appendices
	Sept 13		1st Sept. nown action at W29 d 22	
	14		1.7.6cm T.M. taken up + got into action at E12a 5142	
	15		90 rds fired between 10.45am and Dawn on hostile posts & Flas F5b, F7a	
	16		98 rds fired at train on strongpoints W30 d, W30 c & F6a & F6 c.	
	17		120 rds fired between 2am & 5.30am on strongpoints F4a Elva Wood W30 d &	
	18		275 rds fired on strongpoints between 8pm & 5.20am on strongpoints	
			Jackdaw W30 d 7.3, Wood farm Orchard post Isolero huts Nypher coob &c	
			& Mules, 1. 7.6cm Morton moved forward to support 173 Inf.	
			Brigade to X 25 c 3.8	
			Instructions received to reconnoitre OK'd and the Junction	
	19		Railway from X 26 d 69 to X 27 a 00 to X 26 b 84 & thence NE	
			Trench Morton position from which LIMERICK POST & Commu-	
			nication X 21 d & 22 c could be bombarded.	
	20		Further instructions received relative of T.M. positions to bombard	
			LIMERICK POST and KILDARE POST and to provide protective barrage	
			after capture of these posts by 173rd Inf. Brigade	

Army Form C. 2118.

WAR DIARY (cont)
or
INTELLIGENCE SUMMARY.
(Erase heading not required.)

Place	Date	Hour	Summary of Events and Information	Remarks and references to Appendices
	1918 Sept 23rd		58 DA adm No 173 directed withdrawal of batteries from position and concentration of Batteries at LIERAMONT to receive further orders.	
			58th Div Arty to come under orders of GOC Australian Corps	
	25		Officer detailed to take over 4th Australian AR Posts E 14 & 85 -PERONNE to arrange for X Bty (4 Officers & 53 other ranks) proceeded to IV Army Infantry Mortar	
	26		School at SAILLY FLIBEAUCOURT for V Corps assembling on the 29th inst and dispersing on the 15th October 1918.	

A.R.H......
Captain RA
D.T.M.O. 58 DA

D.T.M.O.
58TH
DIV. ARTILLERY.

War Diary

of the

58th Divisional Trench Mortar Batteries R.A.

for the month of

October 1918

Army Form C. 2118.

WAR DIARY
or
INTELLIGENCE SUMMARY.

58th Divisional Trench Mortar Battery RA
October 1918

(Erase heading not required.)

Instructions regarding War Diaries and Intelligence Summaries are contained in F. S. Regs., Part II. and the Staff Manual respectively. Title pages will be prepared in manuscript.

Place	Date	Hour	Summary of Events and Information	Remarks and references to Appendices
LIERAMONT	3rd		3 NCOs A/290 Brigade RFA to assist	
E.7.c.2.2.	6		7 NCOs sent to 291st Brigade to assist	
	11		Entrained at TINCOURT railhead	
	12"		Detrained at HERSIN - billeted in HERSIN	
HERSIN	13"		1 Officer, 7 other ranks sent for duty at APP huts ST PIERRE	
	15"		O.I.C. (Captain J. Delorey) posted to 3rd Balloon Wing RAF as Observer	
			Captains to command MC into new duties of D.T.M.O.	
	16"		D.T.M.O took over from 24" Divn - moved to BULLY GRENAY	
BULLY GRENAY	17"		2 mobile Stokes Mortar Carriages received from D.A.D.O.S. and 3 cable drums	
	18		Moved by lorries from Bully Grenay to MONTIGNY Sheet 44a O.33.b.4.7.	
	19		Officers and other ranks of X Battery returned from IV Army O.25.b.4.7. Trench Mortar School at SAILLY FLIBEAUCOURT	
			Y Bly, Z mobile Trench Mortars and ammunition received by	
			BACQUERY - keeping in touch with Infantry Brigades during advance	
LANNAY	22nd		X Bty moved from MONTIGNY to LANNAY	

Alfred Ball
Captain RGA
7 Div 58 D/y

Vol 519

58th Div. Arty
Trench Mortar Batteries

War Diary
for the month of
November 1918.

Army Form C. 2118.

58th Duke of Trench Mortar
Batteries R.A.

WAR DIARY
or
INTELLIGENCE SUMMARY
(Erase heading not required.)

November 1918

Place	Date	Hour	Summary of Events and Information	Remarks and references to Appendices
LANNAY	Nov 3rd		O/C D.T.M.O carried out a reconnaissance of the Divisional front for possible Trench Mortar positions	
RONGY	4th	0900	"X" B'y moved from LANNAY to RONGY.	
	7th		200 rds T.M.G received	
			Y B'ty returned from attachment to D.A.C	
			4 Mortars and 120 rounds of Ammn taken up to position reconnoitred at BLEHARIES. - Left Sectn. Headquarters location D25 & 65.65 Sheet 44 N.E.	
			Mortars in action in gardens in rear of H.Q.	
	8th		2 Mortars ready for action on Right Sector Divisional front	
			All mortars withdrawn from positions (on enemy retiring) and concentrated at RONGY upon orders received from 16 Q.R.L. and 90 rds T.M.G and 2 mobile mortars also t	
			Batteries attached to Sections of the D.A.C	
	10th		taken & moved forward remainder of Mortars sub sections being 3 sans left at RONGY under Guard, at billet 23 Rue de L'eglise.	
			Move with D.A.C to WIERS, location K 4 a 5.5.	
	11th		Move from WIERS by road to GRANDGLISE, Sheet 45 G 6 c	

WAR DIARY (cont) or INTELLIGENCE SUMMARY.

Army Form C. 2118.

Title pages November 1916

Place	Date	Hour	Summary of Events and Information	Remarks and references to Appendices
GRANDGLISE	12·		"D"T.M.O awarded M.C.	
G 6 c	16·		"D"T.M.O appointed Town Major, GRANDGLISE	
			"X" Bty Officers attached for duty to 290· Bde R.F.A and "Y" Bty Officers attached	
			for duty to 291st Bde R.F.A	
	20·		6 Gunners transferred to 15" Div. Trench Mortar Batteries.	

W.W.K. Sale
Captain M.C. R.G.A
"D"T.M.O 58· D.I.

D.T.M.O.,
58TH
DIVL. ARTILLERY.
No............
Date 30-11-18

Army Form C. 2118.

WAR DIARY

51st Div Arty
T.M. Bys.

INTELLIGENCE SUMMARY.

(Erase heading not required.)

December 1918

Place	Date	Hour	Summary of Events and Information	Remarks and references to Appendices
GRANDGLISE Sheet 45 G6c	1918 Dec			
	10		Lieut J.I. Tarleton took over duties of Hon. Major, GRANDGLISE Area from Capt A.G. Ball M.C. evacuated to hospital	
	14		4 men (miners) sent to I Corps Concentration Camp for demobilization	
	17		1 man (miner) ditto	
	31		Lieut W.J. Hamlett took over duties of Town Major from Lieut J.I. Tarleton.	

W.J. Hamlett
Lieut R.F.A.
1 DTMO 58 DA

D.T.M.O.
58TH
DIV'L. ARTILLERY.
No.
Date 31-12-1918

WO 95/2995/6

58TH DIVISION

58TH DIVL AMMN COLUMN
JAN 1917 — ~~DEC 191~~
1917 MAY

Box 2995

Army Form C. 2118.

WAR DIARY of 58th J.B.C.
or
INTELLIGENCE SUMMARY
(Erase heading not required.)

January 1917.

Vol 1

Place	Date	Hour	Summary of Events and Information	Remarks and references to Appendices
WINCHESTER.	JAN. 6		Received final orders to mobilize.	
SOUTHAMPTON	26	7.10 pm	H.Q. and No1 Section Embarked. See below —	
	27	9.7pm	H.Q. and No1 Section arrived at HAVRE.	
	28	10.5pm	H.Q. and No1 Section left HAVRE.	
HAVRE.	29	9.7pm	H.Q. and No1 Section 58th arrived MEZEROLLES	
			※ A delay in embarkation now took place, owing to Congestion at HAVRE.	

J.D. McEwen
Lieut. Col. R.F.A.,
Commanding 58th A.C.

War Diary
58th D.A.C.
From   To
1-1-17   31-1-17.
Vol. 1

Sheet 1.

AF C 2118

WAR DIARY of 50th D.A.C.
January 1917.

Vol 2

Place	Date	Hour	Summary of Events and Information	Remarks & References to Appendices
SOUTHAMPTON	3rd	7.30 pm	No 2 Section Embarked at SOUTHAMPTON.	
HARVE	4th	6/c am	No 2 Section arrived HARVE	
SOUTHAMPTON	"	7.15 pm	No 3 Section Embarked at SOUTHAMPTON	
HARVE	5	8.15 am	No 3 Section arrived HARVE	
"	"	6.30 pm	No 2 Section left HARVE	
SOUTHAMPTON	"	7.30 pm	No 4 Section Embarked at SOUTHAMPTON	
HEZEROLLES	6.	4.30 pm	No 2 Section arrived MEZEROLLES	
HARVE	"	7/4 pm	No 3 Section left HARVE.	
"	"	8.15 am	No 4 Section arrived HARVE	
MEZEROLLES	7.	5.30 am	No 3 Section arrived MEZEROLLES	
HARVE	"	7.30 am	No 4 Section left HARVE — 1 officer 7 other Ranks 30 L.D. Horses. joined from 2/2/23 Bde Arty.
MEZEROLLES	8	7¼ pm	No 4 Section arrived MEZEROLLES	
"	9th	2¼ pm	No 4 Section left HEZEROLLES and encamped at OUTREBOIS	
"	(11)		D.A.C. reorganized I.E. H.Q. "A" Echelon 2 Sections and "B" echelon
			Strength :- Officers 15 Other Ranks 696 Ride Horses 76 L.D. 816 Total 892
			293rd A.F.A. B.A.C. formed
"	16th		Strength Officers 3 Other Ranks 142 Ride Horses 21 L.D. 170 Total 191.
			50. G.S. wagon and 50 Pre Horses attached to 29th D.A.C.

Army Form C 2118

Sheet II

WAR DIARY of 58th D.A.C.
February 1917.

PLACE	DATE	HOUR	SUMMARY OF EVENTS AND INFORMATION	Remarks and reference to appendices
MEZEROLLES	18th		New Designation of Sections in accordance with reorganization. 28 Wagons G.S. + Teams 76 attached to Divisional Train. No 3 Section becomes No 1. No 2 Section No change. No 4 Section becomes No 3 Section. "B" Echelon	
"	19th		11 Other Ranks left on posting to Trench Mortar Batteries.	
"	20th		9 Reinforcements arrived from Trench Mortar Batteries.	
"	21st		5 Other Ranks left for duty at Divisional Baths at PAS.	
"	22nd		12 Horses sent to Base Hospital and struck off Strength.	
"	23rd		4 Reinforcements arrived from Trench Mortar Batteries. Lieut A.H. Soulsby assumed Command of No 1 Section vice Capt W.J. LINDSAY FOR 13 F.S. posted to Command 293rd AFA B.A.C. 78 G.S. wagons returned from 58th Div. Train and T9 D.A.C.	
"	24th		D.A.C. moved from MEZEROLLES and OUTRE Bois	
WARLICOURT			H.Q. arrived and encamped at WARLICOURT. No 1 & 2 Sections arrived and encamped at LA BEZEQUE FARM.	
LA BEZEQUE GROUCHES	25th		No 3 Sections + 293rd A.F.A.B.A.C. arrived and billetted for the night at GROUCHES.	
WARLICOURT	27th		No 3 Section arrived and encamped at WARLICOURT.	
LA BEZEQUE	28th		Nos 1 & 2 Sections moved to PAS, and encamped. 293rd A.F.A. B.A.C. ceased to be under attached to D.A.C.	

War Diary
58th D.A.C.

from
1-2-17

to
28-2-17

Volume 2.

Sheet II.

WAR DIARY of 58'D D.A.C.
February 1917.

Army Form C 2118

Summary of Events and Information

PLACE	Date	Hour		Remarks & references to Appendices
MEZEROLLES	1-18.		Weather Cold with frost & snow. Roads in good condition. Variable with rain. A thaw took place rendering the roads in a very bad state. Owing to the bad state of the roads, Mechanical transport was stopped running, consequently a great deal of extra transport had to be done by the D.A.C. and number of horses had to be evacuated. Locality MEZEROLLES The whole area here is undulating and well watered WARLICOURT:- The whole area here is undulating, wooded and fairly good water supply (ii) Roads All except the Main ARRAS Road are in very bad condition	
	19 & 8			

J.V.W... Lieut. Col. R.F.A.
(Lon.) D.A...
Commanding 58th

WAR DIARY.
58th D.A.C.

From. To.
1-2-17 28-2-17

Vol. II

A.F. C 2118

WAR DIARY of 58th D.A.C.
March 1917

Vol 3

Sheet 1.

Summary of Events and Information

Place	Date	Hour	Summary of Events and Information	Remarks & references to appendices
WARLICOURT	1st		3 Officers and 22 Other Ranks proceeded to III Army School of Horses. Lieut. St.FOFCHAK. 18 Drivers, 36 Horses, 6 wagons attached to 507 By R.E. Weather:- Cold with frost at night. Roads in a very bad state.	
	2nd		1 Horse destroyed. Weather:- Dry and cold, frost at night.	
	3rd		4 reinforcements (Gunners) arrived. Two animals dipped. 2/Lieuts. C.H. Brailsford and A.F. Stevens joined. H.R.R.A. moved to BAVICOURT. Weather:- Cold, some snow.	
	4th		1 NCO attended III Army Physical training course. Weather:- Cold, frost at night.	
	5th		2 Drivers & Horses attached to Trench Mortar Bty for ration duty. 1 NCO, 18 Drivers, and 36 horses attached 511 By R.E. Weather:- mild, slight thaw, roads very bad.	
	6th		2 Horses evacuated to M.V.S. Weather:- Mild, thaw continues rendering roads very bad. It is noticed that owing to the bad state of the roads the horses are falling off considerably in condition.	
	9th		3 Officers and 22 Other Ranks returned from Trench Mortar Course. 1 Mule shot. Weather:- Rain and some snow, slight frost at night.	

A.F. C2118

WAR DIARY of 58th D.A.C.
MARCH 1917.

Place	Date	Hour	Summary of Events and Information	Remarks & References to appendices
WARLINCOURT	10th		2 N.C.Os. 15 Gunners and 5 Drivers posted to Trench Mortar Bty. Weather:- mild with some rain. Roads very badly cut up.	
	11th		400 animals inspected by Brig. Gen. FASSON.	
	12th		2/Lieuts. J.L. Myers and R. Grant joined. 1st Reinforcements (2 NCOs 8 Gnrs + 9 Drs) arrived. Weather:- mild.	
	13th		2/Lieut F.R. Brown attended Sanitary Course C.T. POZ.	
	14th		2/Lieut J.L. Myers posted to 290th Bde R.F.A. 2/Lieut S.R. Stillman posted to N.H. Section 58th D.A.C. Weather:- mild with periods of rain.	
	16th		2/Lieut H.S. (Olbery?) posted to 2 T.M. Bty. Lieut K.A.R. Strathman joined from 2/58 T.M.Bty & posted to N.Amm. Section. 58th D.A.C. Capt. the Rev. W.L. NANTON C.F. joined. Weather:- mild. slight frost at night.	
	17th		3 Horses evacuated M.V.S. Debility.	
	18th		12 reinforcements (all Drivers) arrived. Weather:- mild. fine.	
	19th		2/Lieut N. Bonjewater arrived.	
	20th		1 man admitted to Hospital. 1 man proclaimed from Hospital. Weather:- mild.	

AF C2118

WAR DIARY of 56th D.A.C.

Sheet 3

Place	Date	Hour	Summary of Events and Information	Remarks & References to appendices
WARLUCOURT	21st	9pc	No 2 Section moved to BIENVILLIERS. 1 mule died exhaustion. Lieut. F. Atkinson attached 7 H.By. 1 man discharged from hospital. 1 man evacuated sick also 1 mule from 38th Division transferred to VII Corps.	
	22nd		1 man admitted to hospital. 1 man discharged fm hospital.	
	24th		1 man admitted CCS Novo — Struck by lightning /15.	
	26th		Weakened, mild. Man continues. A.D.V.S. inspected animals of No 1 & No 2 Sections. Mules received "to be pushed to more".	

AF C2118

WAR DIARY

Staff IV

of 58th D.A.C.
March 1917.

Place	Date	Hour	Summary of Events & Information	Remarks & References to Appendices
WARLINCOURT			**Horses** Condition of — As noted in my war diary of February 1917 156 horses were led to the Divisional train — these horses were very emaciated when returned and seemingly neglected. This together with the horses loaned to the R.E.'s and the bad state of the roads greatly account as for the number of animals evacuated during the month. **Health** Good — a few cases of German measles. **Weather** Generally cold with snow, many nights frost by, during the middle of the month the roads became very bad rendering transport very difficult	

S. [signature]
Lieut. Col. R.F.A.,
Commanding 58th (Lon.) D.A.C.

A.F. C2118

WAR DIARY
58"D.A.C. April 1917.

Summary of Events and Information

Place	Date	Hour		Remarks & references to appendices
BIENVILLERS	15/4/17	9·15am	left BIENVILLERS.	Cal.
ERVILLERS	15/4/17	3·30pm	arrived ERVILLERS.	Cal.

J.D.L.V.A. Evans.
Lieut. Col. R.F.A.,
Commanding 58th (LOM.) D.A.C.

Vol 5

CONFIDENTIAL
****

WAR DIARY

OF

56th D.A.C.

From 1/5/17
To 28/5/17

WAR DIARY
INTELLIGENCE SUMMARY.
(Erase heading not required.)

Army Form C. 2118.

58th (London) T.R.A.

Place	Date	Hour	Summary of Events and Information	Remarks and references to Appendices
In the field			NIL	

J. D. Royston
Lieut. Col. R.F.A.,
Commanding 58th (Lon.) D.A.G.

WAR DIARY
INTELLIGENCE SUMMARY. 1 30/6/17

Place	Date	Hour	Summary of Events and Information	Remarks and references to Appendices
With Field			58 DAC	
			N/L	

Ewan Kelway
Lieut: & Adjutant,
58th (London) Divisional Ammunition Column.

SECRET. WAR DIARY
INTELLIGENCE SUMMARY.
(Erase heading not required.)

58th (London) Div: Sig:
Month: Ending July 1917

Place	Date	Hour	Summary of Events and Information	Remarks and references to Appendices
In the field	4/7/17		B.A.b. marched from Camp at ERVILLERS-BEHAGNIES:— HQ, No 2 and 3 Sections to "A" Camp FRICOURT No 1 Section accompanied 290 Bde R.F.A. to location near YTRES — Sheet 57c. Arthur 2. V.3.c.4.4.	
In the field	6/7/17		HQ No 2 and 3 Sections marched from "A" Camp FRICOURT to Camp at YTRES – LECHELLE. HQ P31. d.1.8 locations (Sheet 57c Edition '2). No 2 Sec — P25 d.8.6 No 3 Sec — P25 d.5.5 No 1 Section did not move.	

Arthur F. Handy. Capt. R.E.
Comdg (proth) 58th (London) Div: Sig:

SECRET.   Vol 8. Page. 1.

WAR DIARY.

58th (LONDON) Bde - Week Ending 3/8/17.

Summary of Events and Information

Place	Date	Hour		Remarks
	26/8/17		(a) Move of H.Q. Staff, No 1 Section and No 2 Section.	
			H.Q. No 1 Section and No 2 Section marched to ARRAS from locations as under:—	
			H.Q. Staff. } Sheet 51 B. M.17.c.	
			No 1 Section }	
			No 2 Section. Sheet 57 C. A.12.d.7.7.	
	Night of 26-27/8/17		Entrained from ARRAS to POPERINGHE	
	27/8/17		Marched from POPERINGHE to locations as under:—	
			H.Q. Staff } Sheet 28. G.26. a.1.9.	
			No 2 Section }	
			No 1 Section. Sheet 28. G.26. d.0.2	
			(b) Move of No 3 Section	
	27/8/17		Marched to ARRAS from location at M.M.G. Sheet 51 B.	
			And entrained to GODEWAERSVELDE.	
	28/8/17		Marched from GODEWAERSVELDE to location at L.36.C.Central Sheet 27.	

Page 2

WAR DIARY

58th (London) D.A.C. — month ending 31/8/17

Place	Date	Hour	Summary of Events and Information	Remarks
	30/8/17		D.A.C. moved Complete to locations as under :—	
			H.Q. H.31.d.5.1 Sheet 28	
			No 1 Section H.32. c.5.7. "	
			No 2 Section H.32. a.7.4. "	
			No 3 Section H.32. c.7.8. "	

J.D. Lloyd Evans
Lieut. Col. R.F.A.
Commanding 58th (London) D.A.C.

31/8/17 Jo H.Q. R.A.
58th (London) Division.

SECRET.

WAR DIARY

58th (London) D.A.C. — Month ending 30/9/17

Summary of Events and Information

Place	Date	Hour		Remarks

	3/9/17		D.A.C. moved complete from locations as under :-
			
			      H.Q. H.31. d 5.1 (Sheet 28).
			      No1 Sec: H.32. c.5.4 "
			      No 2 " H.32. a 7.4 "
			      No 3 " H.32. c. 7.8 "
			
			 to billets at LE NOUVEAU MONDE (near HERZEELE).
				Vol 9

	7/9/17		D.A.C. moved complete — to relieve 23rd D.A.C. — from LE NOUVEAU MONDE to locations as under :-
			
			      H.Q. A. 30. 6. 9. 7. (Sheet 28)
			      No1 Sec. A. 30. 6. 9. 9. (")
			      No 2 " B. 25 a 3. 3. (")
			      No 3 " B. 26. C. 9.2 (")	

58th R.A. 58th (Lond.) Division 30/9/17.

J.D. Loyd Evans
Lieut. Col. R.F.A.,
Commanding 58th (Lond.) D.A.C.

AF C2118 58

WAR DIARY

58th (London Divl. Ammn Column)

Summary of Events and Information

Place	Date	Hour	
VLAMERTINGHE	2/11/17	7.30 pm	The Column marches from camp in VLAMERTINGHE Area to NORMHOUDT Area.
NORMHOUDT	3/11/17	8 am	The Column marches from NORMHOUDT to RECQUES ARTILLERY Area. HQrs at RUMINGHEM.
RUMINGHEM	12/11/17	8 am	The Column marches to DESVRES AREA. HQrs at DESVRES.
DESVRES	13/11/17	8 am	The Column marches to ESTREE ARTILLERY Area. HQrs at TUBERSENT.
TUBERSENT	14/11/17	2 pm	HQrs. removed to FRENCQ.
FRENCQ	15/11/17	1 pm	HQrs. removed to MARESVILLE.

8/12/17

J.D. Lloyd Evans
Lieut Col RFA
Commanding 58th (Lon) DAC

10 HQRA
58 (Lon) Division

WAR DIARY.

58th (London) Divisional Ammunition Column.

Vol 12

Place	Date	Hour	Summary of Events and Information.	Remarks and References to Appendices
MARESVILLE.	4/12/17	8.80 A.m	The Column marched to THIEMBRONNE Artillery Area, with Headquarters at MERCK-St-LIEVIN.	
MERCK-St-LIEVIN	5/12/17	9 a.m.	The Column marched to LEDERZEELE.	
LEDERZEELE.	6/12/17	9.30 a.m	The Column marched to ZERMEZEELE.	
ZERMEZEELE	7/12/17	7 a.m.	The Column marched to HAMHOEK Artillery Area, with Headquarters located at "X" Camp, A.16.b.5.2. (Sheet 28 N.W.)	
	15/12/17	12 noon	Headquarters moved to ROUSSEL FARM Camp, B.13.a.3.7 (Sheet 28 N.W.)	

J.D.Lloyd Evans Lieut.Col. R.F.A.
Commanding 58th (London) Divnl. Ammn. Col.

To:- A.Q.R.A.
58th (London) Division

1/1/18.

SECRET

Army Form C. 2118.

58th (London) D.A.C.
Month ending 31/1/18.

WAR DIARY
or
INTELLIGENCE SUMMARY.
(Erase heading not required.)

Instructions regarding War Diaries and Intelligence Summaries are contained in F. S. Regs., Part II. and the Staff Manual respectively. Title pages will be prepared in manuscript.

Place	Date	Hour	Summary of Events and Information	Remarks and references to Appendices
—	31/1/18	—	Column marched from ROUSSEL FARM Camp B.13.a.3.4. (Sheet 28 NW.) to Staging Area as under :—	
			H.Q. Staff – PARDO Camp, F.14.c.5.6. (Sheet 27).	
			Nos 1 & 2 Sections – F.24.a.9.3. (Sheet 27).	
			S.A.A. Section – A.19.b.1.8. (Sheet 28).	
—	22-24/1/18	—	Column marched from staging area to PROVEN, then entrained, detrained at VILLERS–BRETONNEUX and marched to Billets at VAIRE.	
—	28/1/18	—	Column marched to new locations as under :—	
			H.Q. Staff and No 2 Section – HERLY	
			No 1 Section – ETALON	
			S.A.A. Section – SEPT-FOURS	
—	29/1/18	—	Column marched to BABOEUF	
—	31/1/18			

J.D. Loyd Evans
Lieut. Col. R.F.A.
Commanding 58th (Lon) D.A.C.

SECRET.

Army Form C. 2118.

WAR DIARY
or
INTELLIGENCE SUMMARY.
(Erase heading not required.)

58 B (London) R.F.A.
Month of February 28-2-18.

Instructions regarding War Diaries and Intelligence Summaries are contained in F. S. Regs., Part II. and the Staff Manual respectively. Title pages will be prepared in manuscript.

Place	Date	Hour	Summary of Events and Information	Remarks and references to Appendices
BABOEUF	6-2-18		Column marched to GENES	

27-2-18
H.Q.R.A.
58th (Lond) Div.

Arthur F Landy. Capt. R.F.A.
Temp. Comdg. 58th (London) Div.

58th (London) D.A.C.

WAR DIARY – March 1918

Date	Hour	Summary of Events or Information	Remarks
22/3/18	1. P.M.	D.A.C. marched from OGNES to new locations as under:— Hq. and S.a.a Section — BABOEUF No. 1 and 2 Sections — MONDESCOURT.	Vol 15 # New 96th B.a.c (½ C.E.) Came under Command of O.C. 58th DAC
23/3/18	5. P.M.	D.A.C. marched, complete, to QUIERZY #	
24/3/18	1.30 P.M.	D.A.C. } marched, complete, to BOURGUIGNON 96th B.A.C. }	
25/3/18	1. P.M.	D.A.C. } marched to new locations as under:— 96th B.A.C. } Hq. to 2 Section, S.a.a Section and 96th BAC – BLERANCOURT No. 1 Section –. CUTS	
26/3/18		No. 1 Section marched to ST PAUL	
27/3/18	12 noon	D.A.C. } marched Complete, to LE MESNIL. 96th BAC } (No. 1 Section via ST AUBIN)	

4 April 1918
Hq. R.a
58th (Lond.) Division

J. D. Lightfoot
Lieut. Col. R.F.A.
Commanding 58th (Lon.) D.A.C.

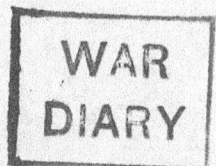

58th DIVISIONAL AMMUNITION COLUMN.

A P R I L

1 9 1 8

SECRET
58

Army Form C. 2118.

WAR DIARY
INTELLIGENCE SUMMARY.
(Erase heading not required.)

58th (London) DAC
April 1918

Place	Date	Hour	Summary of Events and Information	Remarks and references to Appendices
	1-4-18	1 pm	D.A.C. and 96th B.O.C. moved from LE MESNIL to following locations:- HQ. and BAC – CHEVILLE COURT No 1 Sec and S.A.A Section – CHRISTOPHE. A. BERRY No 2 Section – HAUTE BRAYE	9/5/16
	3-4-18	12.15am	D.A.C. and 96th B.A.C. commenced to march to VILLERS COTTERET and LONGPONT to entrain for SALEUX and LONGEAU; hence D.A.C. marched to locations as under, which were occupied by 3.30 pm. 5/4/18:- HQ. – CAGNY : No 1 Section – Bd DE ST QUENTIN, AMIENS: No 2 Section – RUE DE CAGNY, BOUTILLERIE: SAA Section – Iron Foundry, BOUTILLERIE	
	7-4-18	2 pm	D.A.C. less SAA Section marched to locations near GUSY, with HQ at N.26.a.9.9 (Sheet 62 D) to relieve 16th DAC – on relief, coming under orders of 5th Australian D.A. Notification received – 58th HQRA memo ADA 146 d/5.4.18 that SAA Section controlled by 58th Div "Q".	
	11-4-18	2 pm	DAC less SAA Section marched to locations near LAMOTTE (N. of SOMME R) into HQ at N.8.d.3.2. (Sheet 62 D)	

SECRET

WAR DIARY
of
INTELLIGENCE SUMMARY. 58th (London) D.A.C. — May 1918

Army Form C. 2118.

Vol 17

Place	Date	Hour	Summary of Events and Information	Remarks and references to Appendices
EAUCOURT SUR SOMME	4/5/18	9 a.m.	S.A.A. Section, 58 DAC marched from EAUCOURT-SUR-SOMME and joined 173rd Infy Bde Transport Column at BOURDON	
BOURDON	7/5/18	8.30 a.m.	S.A.A. Section marched from BOURDON to present location near CONTAY. C.3. central (Sheet 62 D)	
EAUCOURT SUR SOMME	10/5/18	9 a.m.	HQ, Section 1 and Section 2, 58 DAC marched from EAUCOURT-SUR-SOMME and entered Billets at BELLOY	
BELLOY	11/5/18	6.30 a.m.	HQ, Section 1 and Section 2. 58 DAC marched from BELLOY to present locations as under:—	
			HQ. — CONTAY. Billet No 24	
			No 1 Section — B.6.d.15. (Sheet 62.D) near BEAUCOURT.	
			" 2 " T.29.c.6.2 (Sheet 57 D).	
CONTAY	24/5/18		Major C. HARRIS (D.O.) R.A. assumed Command of 58th DAC vice Lt. Col. J.D. Lloyd-Evans, R.F.A. (to England) 24/5/18.	
	31/5/18		H.Q.R.A. 58th (Lond) Divn	

Major (S.O.) R.A.
Comdg. 58th (London) D.A.C.

Secret

Army Form C. 2118.

WAR DIARY
INTELLIGENCE SUMMARY.
(Erase heading not required.)

58th (London) D.A.C.
Month ending 30 June 1918.

W.D. /8

Place	Date	Hour	Summary of Events and Information	Remarks and references to Appendices
CONTAY	8/6/18	9 a.m.	S.A.A. Section marched from CONTAY to B.Q.C. - (Sheet 62 D) near MOLLIENS-AU-BOIS and passed under orders of "Q", 58th Div.	
CONTAY	9/6/18	10.30 a.m.	D.A.C. less S.A.A Section marched from CONTAY and entered billets at LONGPRÉ.	
B.Q.C.	10/6/18	8.30 a.m.	S.A.A. Section marched to PICQUIGNY.	
LONGPRÉ	10/6/18	6.15 a.m.	D.A.C. less S.A.A Section marched from LONGPRÉ and entered billets at BEHENCOURT with Headquarters at the Chateau.	
PICQUIGNY	20/6/18	7.30 a.m.	S.A.A. Section marched (still under orders of "Q") from PICQUIGNY to C.3 Central - (Sheet 62 D) near CONTAY.	
	24/6/18	noon	S.A.A. Came under orders of O.C. 58th D.A.C.	
	30/6/18		H.Q. R.A. 58th (London)	

[signature] MAJOR, (D.O.) R.A.
COMDG. 58TH (L) D.A.C.

SECRET

Army Form C. 2118.

WAR DIARY
INTELLIGENCE SUMMARY.
(Erase heading not required.)

58th (London) Div.
Month ending 31st July 1918

Instructions regarding War Diaries and Intelligence Summaries are contained in F. S. Regs., Part II. and the Staff Manual respectively. Title pages will be prepared in manuscript.

Place	Date	Hour	Summary of Events and Information	Remarks and references to Appendices
H.Q. R.A. 58th (Lond) Divn.	31/7/18		NIL RETURN	

[Signed] J Dawes
MAJOR, (D.O.) R.A.
COMDG. 58TH (L) D.A.C.

58th Divl. Artillery

58th DIVISIONAL AMMUNITION COLUMN,

A U G U S T   1 9 1 8.

SECRET.

Army Form C. 2118.

WAR DIARY
INTELLIGENCE SUMMARY.
(Erase heading not required.)

Instructions regarding War Diaries and Intelligence Summaries are contained in F. S. Regs., Part II. and the Staff Manual respectively. Title pages will be prepared in manuscript.

58th (London) Div.
Month ending 31/8/18.
Vol 20

Place	Date	Hour	Summary of Events and Information	Remarks and references to Appendices
near CONTAY	3/8/18	9.30 am	LAA section moved from C.3 Central, near CONTAY (Sheet 62 D)	
			to QUERRIEU and came under orders of "Q" 58th (Lond) Divn	
BEHENCOURT	8/8/18	10.30 am	" " LAA section moved to LA NEUVILLE (SOMME) - Sheet 62 D	
LA NEUVILLE	9/8/18	2.30 pm	" " to location I.23.d.Central, near BONNAY Sheet 62 D	
BONNAY	12/8/18	9 am	" " to location J.34.b.5.3, near SAILLY-le-SEC, Sheet 62 D	
SAILLY-le-SEC	27/8/18	8.30 am	" " to location E.18.central near MEAULTE, Sheet 62 D	
MEAULTE	28/8/18	8.30 am	" " to location K.24.a.6.3 near ETINEHEM, Sheet 62 D	
ETINEHEM	29/8/18	8 am	" " to location A.28.b.7.5, near MARICOURT, Sheet 62 C.	

31/8/18 HQ RA
         58th (Lond) Division

C. Harris
MAJOR, (D.) R.A.
COMDG. 58TH (L) L.A.O.

SECRET

WAR DIARY
INTELLIGENCE SUMMARY

Army Form C. 2118.

58th (London) Dab.
Week ending 30th September/18

Place	Date	Hour	Summary of Events and Information	Remarks and references to Appendices
nr MARICOURT	5/9/18	6.30pm	D.A.C. less I.a.a. Section moved from A.28.c.7.5 (Sheet 62 c), near MARICOURT, to location near CLERY sur SOMME with HQ at H.6.d.8.0 (Sheet 62 c)	
CLERY s.SOMME	6/9/18	1.30pm	D.A.C., less I.a.a. Section moved to near ALLAINES with HQ at I.3.d.cent (" ")	
ALLAINES	9/9/18	9am	D.A.C. less I.a.a Section moved to near MOISLAINS with HQ at D.2.cent (" ")	
			Note: I.a.a. Section still under orders of "Q" 58th Division	

30/9/18
HQ Rd. 58th (Lond) Div.

[signature]
MAJOR, (D.O.) R.A.
COMDG. 58TH (L) D.A.C.

SECRET.

WAR DIARY
-of-
INTELLIGENCE SUMMARY.
(Erase heading not required.)

Army Form C. 2118.

58th (London) D.A.C.
Month ending 31st October 1918.

Place	Date	Hour	Summary of Events and Information	Remarks and references to Appendices
in MOISLAINS	9/10/18	0630	D.A.C. (less 1 a/c section) moved from in MOISLAINS (D.2. cent. Sheet 62B) to location nr BONY (Sheet 62B).	9/11 22
nr. BONY	9/10/18	1100	D.A.C. (less 1 a/c section) moves from nr BONY (Sheet 62B), to location nr. DRIENCOURT (Sheet 62c).	
nr. DRIENCOURT	10/10/18	1000	D.A.C. (less 1 a/c section) commenced to entrain from PERONNE and TINCOURT to 1st First Army —	
	12/10/18		Detrainment completed and locations occupied as under — HQrs. BULLY GRENAY. No 1 Section HERSIN. No 2 Section MOROC.	Sheet 11 (LENS)
BULLY GRENAY	13/10	1100	HQrs moved to HERSIN.	
MOROC	"	0920	No 2 Section moved to HERSIN.	(Sheet 44A)
HERSIN	18/10	1130	D.A.C. (less 1 a/c section) moved to Ferm du BARLET nr MONTIGNY.	
MONTIGNY	19/10	1130	ditto to EVIN - MALMAISON.	do
EVIN	20/10	1030	ditto to LA VACQUERIE.	do
LA VACQUERIE	21/10	0930	ditto to LANNAY	Sheet 44
			Note. 1 a/c section still under orders of 58th Div. "Q"	

J Harris
MAJOR, (D.O.) R.A.
COMDG. 58TH (L) D.A.C.

58th (London) D.A.C. R.F.A.

Army Form C. 2118.

WAR DIARY
or
INTELLIGENCE SUMMARY.
(Erase heading not required.)

Instructions regarding War Diaries and Intelligence Summaries are contained in F. S. Regs., Part II. and the Staff Manual respectively. Title pages will be prepared in manuscript.

Place	Date	Hour	Summary of Events and Information	Remarks and references to Appendices
LANNAY	9/11/18	1400	Column (Head A.A. Section) moved to location near RONCQ	I.11.c cent. (Sheet
nr. RONCQ	10/11/18	1030	Column (less 1 A.A. Section) moved to LE CROIX nr. WIERS K.3.d.	(Sheet 44)
LE CROIX	11/11/18	0930	Column (less 1 A.A. Section) moved to GRANDGLISE	H.6.c. (Sheet45)
ST AMBROSE	12/11/18	0900	1 A.A. Section moved to GRANDGLISE and came under orders of O.C. 58th (London) D.A.C.	

To :- H.Q.R.A.
58th (London) Div.

[signature]
MAJOR, (D.O.) R.A.
COMDG. 58TH (L) D.A.C.

58th (London) D.A.C

Army Form C. 2118.

WAR DIARY
or
INTELLIGENCE SUMMARY.
(Erase heading not required).

Instructions regarding War Diaries and Intelligence Summaries are contained in F. S. Regs., Part II. and the Staff Manual respectively. Title pages will be prepared in manuscript.

Place	Date	Hour	Summary of Events and Information	Remarks and references to Appendices
GRANDGLISE	1/12/18	—	Major C. Harris MC, DCM, (DORA), proceeds on leave to U.K. —	
do.	1/12/18	—	Captain W. Toulza M.C., R.F.A., assumes temporary command during the absence of Major C. Harris.	

3/12/18
To:- H.Q.R.A.,
58th (London) Division.

J.W.Toulza
Capt. R.F.A.
Temp. Comdg.: 58th (London) D.A.C

[Stamp: 58TH (LONDON) DIVISION AMMUNITION COLUMN No. 74/9 1 JAN 1919]

WAR DIARY
or
INTELLIGENCE SUMMARY.

Army Form C. 2118.

58th (London) D.A.C. R.F.A.

Summary of Events and Information

Nothing to record during April, 1919.

1-5-19

To HQrs. 58th Div. front.

J.M. Mronpe Capt.
R.F.A.,
Commanding 58th (Lon.) D.A.C.

WAR DIARY or INTELLIGENCE SUMMARY.

Army Form C. 2118.

58 (Lond) DAC 29

58th (London) DAC

Place	Date	Hour	Summary of Events and Information	Remarks and references to Appendices
BELBEIH	1 to 31/5/19		Nothing to record during the month	
	3/5/19		To:- H.Q. 58th Div: Amm.	

H.W. Moule Capt.
R.F.A.,
Commanding 58th (Lond) DAC

www.ingramcontent.com/pod-product-compliance
Lightning Source LLC
Chambersburg PA
CBHW082007220426
43670CB00014B/2573